Date Due

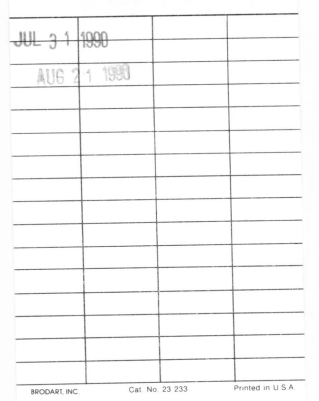

Letters to a Québécois Friend

Philip Resnick

with a reply by Daniel Latouche

McGill-Queen's University Press
Montreal & Kingston • London • Buffalo

© McGill-Queen's University Press 1990
ISBN 0-7735-0772-8 (cloth)
ISBN 0-7735-0777-9 (paper)

Legal deposit first quarter 1990
Bibliothèque nationale du Québec

Printed in Canada

Reprinted 1990

Canadian Cataloguing in Publication Data
Resnick, Philip, 1944–
Letters to a Québécois friend
ISBN 0-7735-0772-8 (bound) –
ISBN 0-7735-0777-9 (pbk.)
1. Resnick, Philip, 1944– – Correspondence. 2. Canadians,
English-speaking – Correspondence. 3. Latouche, Daniel,
1945– – Correspondence. 4. Canadians, French-speaking –
Quebec (Province) – Correspondence. 5. Quebec (Province)
– Politics and government – 1960–   . 6. Canada –
English-French relations. 7. Canada – Politics and
government – 1963–1984. 8. Canada – Politics and
government – 1984–   . I. Latouche, Daniel,
1945–   . II. Title.
FC630.R47 1990   971.4'04
C90-090014-8   F1034.2.R47 1990

Contents

To the Reader

These letters were written *en bloc* in December 1988 to an imaginary Québécois friend in the immediate aftermath of the November 1988 federal election and as the controversy over the Supreme Court judgment on language signs was swirling in Quebec. As fate would have it, they will appear in print more than twelve months later, and with a response by Daniel Latouche to which I would not, of course, have been privy at the time of writing. Much has happened over the past year that suggests a hardening of attitudes in both English Canada and Quebec and a corresponding tendency for the two to drift apart. Public opinion polls show this change, as does the 1989 Quebec election result. There is increased polarization around Meech Lake, language rights, and our respective commitment to Canada as a country.

In the text that follows, the reader will not find me addressing the most recent developments or responding directly to the points that Daniel Latouche raises. (That would require a reply at least as lengthy as his own.) Instead, these letters, essentially unchanged from when they were first written, faithfully capture the reflections of an English-speaking Canadian who has been more than sympathetic to Quebec nationalism in the past. Yet he now finds himself, in light of both the free trade debate and Bill 178, forced to rethink his position fundamentally.

The tone I have adopted ranges from the analytical and fairly objective to the emotional and passionate. On the one hand, I want to begin a dialogue with my Québécois friend based on certain historical and contemporary realities that we both need to examine. On the other, I am as much touched by English Canadian nationalism and our own struggle for a distinct identity as any Québécois nationalist may be touched by that of Quebec. Still, my principal goal has been to stretch out a hand to *mes amis québécois* rather than to slam doors in their faces. These letters seek to speak directly to our present predicament in a way that leaves the future open. At the same time, they testify to the wrenching reassessment which the policies pursued by the Mulroney and Bourassa governments are imposing on this country.

Philip Resnick
Vancouver, December 1989

Letters to a Québécois Friend

Philip Resnick

Where do I begin? The election of 21 November 1988 is over. Parliament has been convened; the passage of the Canada–United States Trade Agreement is but a matter of weeks. The agreement will carry because the government which will put it through received a bare 40 per cent of the popular vote and a minority of the seats in Canada outside Quebec and a clear majority of the popular vote (53 per cent) and 63 of the 75 seats in that province. Nothing terribly exceptional about your providing the decisive margin for a federal party to form a majority government in Ottawa. A similar margin kept the Liberals in power during their long tenure from Wilfrid Laurier to Pierre Elliott Trudeau; so there seems no particular reason, other than partisan disappointment, to deny Brian Mulroney's Conservatives their turn.

And yet, *cher ami* (and you are a friend, or even closer, what Baudelaire might have termed *un semblable, un frère*), something has changed in my sentiments towards you and, I fear, those of many English-speaking Canadians, something which will leave an indelible mark on this country for a generation or more. A feeling of profound hurt has come over many of us, especially those who, in the recent past, were most sympathetic to Quebec and its national aspirations. The feeling, quite simply, is one of betrayal.

That is a strong word with which to begin these epistles, and I know already how you will instinctively react to such an accusation. "Betrayal of what?" you will hurl back at me. "Of our own destiny as a people? Of our own hopes for national self-realization, hopes so terribly dashed in the referendum battle of 1980 in which English Canada and all its elites, political no less than economic, made clear their position when Quebec's future as a potentially sovereign entity was the question. No, *mon cher Canadien anglais*, do not come preaching your anguish and woe in the aftermath of your own referendum defeat. There is a justice in the world that has meted out what you so richly deserve."

I am tempted to respond in kind, to voice my rage at your wilful ignoring of our deepest sentiments on free trade, at your total selfishness where Meech Lake is concerned, at the posturing that has come to characterize your claim to some monopoly on nationalist sentiment. As though *you* were the wretched of the earth and your status within Canada in any way comparable to that of minority peoples around the world denied the most elementary of freedoms and rights.

But I will refrain from venting my spleen at so early a stage in our correspondence. How quickly recriminations can replace dialogue on both sides. How easily each reaches for arguments that are closest to hand, affirming what seems most important to his or her own identity, blotting out what gives the other meaning. Already I can feel the two solitudes closing in, the intransigence of divided peoples, belligerent cultures and languages, looming.

I will not take pen in hand simply to spit out Dantesque hatred churned up from the lower reaches of poetic indignation. For, in truth, I do not hate you; I have never hated you, *cher ami*, nor do I wish to beat the tribal drums of English Canada in answer to your own. I have something else in mind, a desire to speak to you in a way in which you have probably never been spoken to before. For what is really at stake in the betrayal that I and so many others feel today is the desire for recognition, for some acknowledgment by you of the kind of society and people *we* really are.

This may seem a strange request directed at Québécois who themselves not so long ago looked for recognition from the rest of Canada, and who to this day feel their survival as a society to be under continual threat. "What is there to recognize about English-speaking Canadians?" you might be tempted to answer. "They inhabit the northern part of this continent, have a way of life and standard of living similar to that of the United States, have had a stranglehold over federal institutions from the time of Confederation, and by and large have been free to get on with their lives as best they choose. If they are colourless and reserved compared to Americans, defensive about a culture which, with one or two exceptions, has produced little of originality or worth, what fault is it of ours? And why should we be asked to care about Toronto or Halifax or Vancouver when our own future is so problematic? A once-conquered people cannot be expected to carry the burden, psychic or otherwise, of its one-time conqueror?"

I want, however, to probe beneath the surface of these old hostilities. And I want to suggest that the problem of recognition is not a one-way street, as many in your society have assumed. If I may invoke, for a moment, Hegel's famous metaphor of the master-slave relationship (and in the 1960s many of your leading artists and intellectuals saw themselves in a slave situation vis-à-vis anglophone colonial masters), then the "master," no less than the "slave," aspires to recognition. Not that I see our relationship today as anything other than one between two free and equal societies. But without mutual recognition there can be no moving forward, no certainty that the self-awareness the one society achieves is not at the expense of the other.

In a strange way, I think the historical tables have been turned, that today it is English-speaking Canada which craves understanding from you and you who collectively turn your back. Where once a more British-oriented Canada cavalierly went its way, ignoring your national sentiments during the Boer and two world wars, imposing its language on French-speaking minorities scattered the length and breadth of the country, controlling your economy through the anglophone minority in Quebec, the last three decades have brought significant change. Beginning with the Quiet Revolution, English Canadians increasingly were forced to come to terms with the question, "What does Quebec want?" And much of our national politics and of your own, over the next twenty years, was taken up with attempting to resolve that question.

In further letters, there will be occasion to go back over that period. For the moment, let me underline a few of the ways in which English Canada has changed, ways which I am not sure you have been prepared to acknowledge. I am not referring here to superficial features like Sunday laws or restaurants, which ads in the Montreal metro boosting Ontario tourism not so long ago emphasized ("Come see how Ontario has changed"). No, I am talking about fundamental attitudes, towards language, culture and the self-definition of this country.

I know, my friend, with what disdain many of the more nationalist in Quebec received the Report of the Royal Commission on Bilingualism and Biculturalism, the subsequent Official Languages Act, and the moves towards greater bilingualism in the federal civil service. These were but attempts to undercut the appeal of nationalism within Quebec, to provide a mythic pan-Canadian context for a language and culture whose ultimate survival was grounded in Quebec. Bilingual airport signs or corn-flakes boxes or radio and television service across the country were no alternative to a French-speaking Quebec, preferably sovereign. Nor did the sudden infatuation with French immersion and the hundreds of thousands of young anglophones registering in such schools from St John's to Victoria provoke more than cynical amusement.

I will admit to having held something of a minority opinion on the issue of second-language instruction and use myself, to having been attracted by a Swiss-type solution to our linguistic problems. There is no right to German-language schools in

Geneva or French-language ones in Zurich, no nonsense about bilingualism within the different cantons; instead, one finds a clear territorial basis for language unsullied by individual language rights. Did it not make sense to go the same route in Canada?

It might have, if Cartesian logic rather than Canadian pragmatism had prevailed. True, there would have been losers: the anglophone minority in Quebec, forced to give up many of its long-established institutions, such as schools, hospitals, radio and television stations; and francophones outside Quebec, condemned to almost certain assimilation within another generation or two. But this way each majority culture – French within Quebec, English in the other nine provinces – would have been free to develop with minimal accommodation to the other. Only at the federal level, within the national capital area, would a certain measure of bilingualism have been required. Otherwise, Canada would have been made up of two unilingual societies, with negligible rights for linguistic minorities within either.

When one thinks the problem through, however, one becomes aware of the high sociological price one would be asking the minorities to pay to secure linguistic and cultural peace for the two majorities. Anglophones in Quebec, many of whom can trace their origins in that province back through many generations, would have had no choice, if they were to continue to live and function in English, but to pick up and leave (as many did through the 1960s and 1970s). Francophones in Manitoba, Ontario, or New Brunswick, if they were serious about the continued use of their language, would have been wise to abandon their provinces of birth and migrate to Quebec. We would have seen a population transfer, hopefully without the bloodshed that transpired on the Indian sub-continent in 1947–8 or more recently in the conflict between Armenia and Azerbaijan, but with only insignificant minorities remaining in each society.

Was this the best option? Thinking about it today, I have serious doubts. We live in a world where minorities of all sorts

– linguistic, racial, religious – exist within the boundaries of nation-states. And we are increasingly conscious of just how often minorities are deprived of the most basic human rights – to political representation, education in their own language, religious practice, social services, and employment. Why would we want to build a society based on principles other than toleration and a broad notion of rights?

This is not an argument against the right of majorities, for example francophones in Quebec to measures to protect and promote their language, or English-speaking Canadians in the rest of Canada to continue to live in a society with English as the dominant language. But it is an argument for a more open and ultimately pluralistic vision of a country than a purely territorial notion of language rights would permit.

The consequences in English Canada of the changes of the past two decades have been important. I do not mean by this that most English-speaking Canadians have become bilingual or are likely to (though a significant minority of younger Canadians will acquire a better knowledge of French than was true before). Nor has the extension of French-language radio or television service to the whole country given it a huge audience outside Quebec. Of course not. But in a subtle way, a majority of English-speaking Canadians have come to accept the French fact as a crucial feature of the Canadian mosaic, as something which makes us indisputably different from the United States. From our leadership debates during elections which are now conducted first in French and then in English, to a whole range of federal government services, to the labelling and packaging of goods, the notion of a Canada with two official languages has taken hold. It has become part of the identity of Canada, domestically and internationally (one thinks of la francophonie), in a way that would have been inconceivable in an earlier period.

Do not get me wrong. I do not want to suggest that Quebec is here being held hostage to English Canada's own search for identity, that your linguistic distinctiveness is the fig leaf with which we can cover our nakedness. There is more to English-speaking Canada than that, as I shall explain. All I want to argue here is that the peculiar version of bilingualism and biculturalism that was adopted, for all its flaws and hidden political motives, has had consequences in shaping our identity. The English Canada of today is not fundamentally hostile to Quebec's survival as a distinct sociological community on this continent in the way that the Loyalists or Orangemen of yore might have been. Nor does the assimilationist impulse of the Durham Report run strong, except perhaps in isolated backwaters of English Canada. To use the title of a film on aging veterans of the Spanish Civil War, *La guerre est finie*. We need to look long and hard at new realities as we move towards the twenty-first century.

All is not admiration and accommodation, to be sure, where attitudes in English Canada towards Quebec are concerned. And the inevitable pull of regionalism will ensure that major decisions which pit an English Canadian province against Quebec, such as the allocation of the CF-18, contract, may take on nationalist overtones. What I want to emphasize is a fundamental acceptance of the French fact as a necessary and desirable feature of Canadian society at large, and this by broad sections of opinion in English Canada.

Take this statement for what it is worth. Discount it, if you wish, as but poor consolation for the waning of the dream of a sovereign Quebec, as the triumph of the federalist ideology of that arch-enemy of Quebec nationalism, Pierre Elliott Trudeau. But please remember that the originator of the notion of bilingualism and biculturalism was a man whose nationalist credentials were impeccable, André Laurendeau, and that its realization has fulfilled the dreams of earlier *French Canadian* nationalists going back to Henri Bourassa. And remember also, whatever your resentments and second thoughts, that for English Canada the Official Languages Act and all that has followed represented a significant accommodation to the linguistic and cultural specificity of Quebec.

More may be required. And we have already seen in the "distinct society" clause of the 1987 Meech Lake Accord a possible move in that direction. And though Meech Lake is now in trouble, for reasons I shall go into another time, the fact remains that there is in English Canada a willingness to take Quebec on its own terms and treat its national aspirations seriously.

What is much less clear is whether Quebec is similarly willing to take English Canada and its national aspirations seriously. Indeed, it is precisely because that willingness seems to me so lacking that I have decided to write these letters. If you read them, perhaps you will discover some of the features that make English Canada a distinct society. And perhaps, just perhaps, we will begin to be able to think about a better future, a more communitarian one, for our two societies.

Yesterday, the Supreme Court ruled on Bill 101, striking down the French-only provisions regarding the language of signs in Quebec. Already the Mouvement québécois français, the Société Saint-Jean-Baptiste, and others have begun to rally and an article in *Le Devoir* refers to Wolfe's second victory over Montcalm. Is this the right day to invoke questions of English Canada's identity, to pass over the new wave of nationalist fervour about to unfold in Quebec?

I can hardly ignore your nationalism, nor is the purpose of these letters to make you drop your commitment to your identity the better to understand our own. But let me focus, for a moment, on the passion with which you resist linguistic and cultural assimilation and ask you whether you are the only people in Canada obsessed with survival as a distinct society.

The simple fact of the matter is that you are not. If there is one group that has claims to distinctiveness that predate both yours and ours, it is clearly the aboriginal peoples of Canada. True, they have been beaten back by the force of arms, by the laws of commerce, by the sheer weight of numbers, so that, by whatever definition we use, they represent today but a bare 2 per cent of the total Canadian population, trying to hold on as best they can in a larger white society not of their own making. The fact that we are still years away from comprehensive land-claim settlements in British Columbia and Alberta, that in northern Quebec the priorities of electricity development have won out over the Crees' way of life, suggests just how far we are from extending the same passionate defence to the rights of these people as we do to our own.

But let me move on from the aboriginal peoples with respect to whom we both have unpaid historical debts, to say something about the English Canadian strand, to which has been joined a multiplicity of groups of diverse origin. I stress this admixture, because English-speaking Canada is indeed culturally diverse (in a way which French-speaking Canada is for the first time showing signs of becoming), and there is nothing racial (as opposed to linguistic) about my use of the term English. How could it be otherwise, when I can no more trace my ancestry to the British than you, when I know full well, moreover, where a purely racial definition of nationalism landed Germany and much of Europe a mere half-century ago?

The British conquest, however, had a dramatic impact on the northern half of this continent. It ensured, at the time of the American Revolution, that not all of British North America would necessarily be caught up in what was to become the United States. Some, at least, of those who rejected the revolutionary break with Britain and the new republican faith, would take up residence to the north of New England and the Great Lakes, populating the Maritimes, the Eastern Townships, Montreal, and what was to become Upper Canada. This would entail the co-existence, side by side, of the English and French, as a permanent feature of these new British colonies.

I must confess to having ambiguous feelings about the Loyalists, with their credo of king and Union Jack and their fervent belief in the hierarchical constitution of Great Britain, with its studious rejection of democratic virtues. (We are, after all, talking about the unreformed constitution before 1832, in which only a tiny fraction of the adult male population had the franchise, and great aristocratic families, be they Whig or Tory, dominated.) And, I must say, I find it much easier to identify with the American revolutionaries of 1776, with the stirring language of Jefferson's Declaration of Independence ("We hold these truths to be self-evident, that all men are created equal"), with the constitutional handiwork of the founding fathers ("We the people of the United States..."), or with the American Bill of Rights ("Congress shall make no law respecting an establishment of religion, or preventing the free exercise thereof"), than with the dull colonial reality of late eighteenth century British North America. Nor can I take enormous pride in the Constitutional Act of 1791 or the Act of Union of 1840, which itself was a direct consequence of the defeat of the Rebellions of 1837, the one and only attempt at revolution in the Canadas. I have always regretted the fact that our country lacks the revolutionary tradition of the United States or France, and I am convinced that we have paid a high price for this in our political culture, on both sides, English and French.

Yet I am not interested here in rewriting history to suit my own purposes. I am prepared to recognize that the Loyalist strand, counter-revolutionary though it was, tied to a British empire for which I, like you, *cher ami*, can feel little enthusiasm, provided the basis for the attempt to build a somewhat different society on the English-speaking side of what was to become Canada than was to be found south of the border. The society in question would be more ordered, more respectful of established religious norms and values, and less passionately individualistic and liberal than the American. And in its own way, it paralleled the more conservative set of values that prevailed in French Canadian society in the high age of ultramontanism, a period in which liberal values were associated with the Jacobins, the French Revolution, 1848, and beyond. I am not the first to recognize this common counter-revolutionary element to our two societies, for all the difficulties this may pose to those of more radical views, like myself or you, a century later.

Just as you found in ultra-catholic values and the rejection of modernity the tools of a certain cultural defence, so did conservative, monarchical values serve a similar purpose on the English Canadian side. Our forefathers may not have used the term "Je me souviens." The commitment to remain attached to Great Britain and, more especially, to refuse absorption into the

United States was, however, as much of a passion for English-speaking Canadians at the time of Confederation and after as your own concerns with survival. Indeed, it is a *leitmotif* of Canadian nationalism from that period to today.

Another element in Confederation had an impact worth emphasizing. For you in Quebec, the sense of nation was already implanted by the period of the Conquest. And there had been in the nineteenth century movements like the Patriotes and the Rouges that articulated it in the political arena. The year 1867 did not represent the sudden birth of a French Canadian identity *ex ovo*. It simply acknowledged that identity by undoing the Act of Union and giving the new province of Quebec significant control over areas such as education and property and civil rights, of greatest concern to its francophone elites and population.

For anglophones, on the other hand, Confederation provided the framework for the creation, slowly and over time, of a new identity. To speak of an English Canadian or Canadian nation in 1867 would strain reality. At best, there now emerged a federal government, or, if one prefers, a Canadian state, which, while short of full independence in a number of important respects (foreign relations, defence, constitutional amendment and interpretation), did nonetheless bring new and important powers to bear on the tasks of nation building. These were most important in the economic realm – a stable currency, the ability to secure loans from abroad (and reassure British investment houses), railway construction, and tariff protection through John A. Macdonald's National Policy. But at the symbolic level as well, the new Dominion of Canada, as it was termed, would gradually become for English-speaking Canadians a pole of loyalty at least as powerful as any strictly regional one. The federal government thus helped to instil a sense of nation where none had existed before.

Without tarrying in post-Confederation history, let me emphasize the quite different perspective anglophones and francophones were to develop on the federal constitution created in 1867. For French Canadians, the crucial event was the emergence of a province enjoying substantial autonomy within which they were assured of permanent control. For English-speaking Canadians, it was the federal government which became the forger and harbinger of identity. This difference in perspective would emerge time and time again throughout our history, during periods of war and economic crisis like the Great Depression and in the more recent period since the Quiet Revolution as well. The passion which you reserve for the government of Quebec many in English-speaking Canada have reserved for the government of Canada.

"Banalités, des lieux communs," I hear you murmuring. "We have known for a long time that you were centralizers at heart, that, without Quebec, federalism would have taken on much more of a top-down form, that only our vigilance has prevented you from making a mockery of the distribution of powers under the British North America Act. Do not attempt to sweet-talk us by calling the federal state the forger of your identity. That simply gives us additional reason to see in it an instrument potentially dangerous to our own."

Well put, my friend, though you are simply repeating certain *lieux communs* on your side. What I am trying to drive home is that our sense of nation is in many ways rooted in the federal government you so disdain, that without that central state there really cannot be a Canadian (or English Canadian) nation. Over the century and a quarter since Confederation, our symbols of nationhood have been associated with it. From mounted police to railway projects to armed forces to national broadcasting, social programs, or the flag, the route for English Canadians has entailed use of that state. To weaken or dismantle it is to strike a blow at our identity.

There is another feature of this state worth drawing to your attention: its role in helping to ward off the threat of wholesale absorption by the United States. You may think I exaggerate, that the United States has had other imperial missions to pursue than the absorption of Canada. You might also suggest that, for all the feigned anti-American sentiment in Ontario or occasionally the Maritimes, the majority of Canadian workers and businessmen and farmers, especially in the West, were far more drawn to the United States, that millions of English Canadians (like hundreds of thousands of French Canadians) were to make the ultimate commitment of physically migrating across the border.

Let me be frank and suggest that there has been a schizophrenic quality to English Canada's attitudes towards the United States, not unlike your own schizophrenic attitudes to the nation-state called Canada. We have been attracted by the United States, its economic dynamism, its cultural energy, its colossal power in world affairs. We have simultaneously feared that its economic might would engulf us, doubted whether its global power was always used wisely, found features of its political culture, from McCarthyism and institutionalized racism to its chauvinism and high rates of violent crime, repugnant in the extreme. And we have sought, sometimes for conservative and counter-revolutionary reasons, sometimes for more egalitarian and communitarian ones, such as regional equalization programs or medicare, to create a different kind of society.

We have gone through different phases in our attitudes towards the United States. The British motif of loyalty to empire prevailed down to 1914 and was, along with hard-nosed business interest, at the heart of the sentimental rallying against reciprocity in the 1911 election in which Laurier's Liberals went down to defeat. World War I, with its tremendous bloodletting on all sides, its 65,000 Canadian soldiers (essentially English Canadian) killed and 150,000 injured, its poor British generalship in the fields of France, did much to foster stronger desires for Canadian autonomy. This feeling was to find expression in the Treaty of Versailles, in Canada's admission to separate membership in the League of Nations. In the 1920s we were to refuse entanglement in overseas British affairs (the Chanak Crisis), to exchange our own ambassadors with the United States, France, and a number of other countries, and to begin to negotiate and sign treaties in our own name. The 1931 Statute of Westminster formalized the independence of the dominions from Great Britain in foreign affairs, something which would be reinforced by the permanent weakening of British power and the break-up of its empire in the aftermath of World War II.

Towards the United States, conversely, our ties began to strengthen, even as those with Britain declined. As Canada, in Harold Innis's words, moved "from colony to nation to colony," there was an increasingly American or North American motif to our political economy and culture. If the Conservatives of Macdonald or Robert Borden or R.B. Bennett had symbolized the old pro-British sense of nationalism, the Liberal Party of Laurier, Mackenzie King, Louis St Laurent and L.B. Pearson came to incarnate a more pro-American pole in Canadian consciousness.

An old reflex was at work, one which had served Canada relatively well as a model of development, namely the linking of our star to the ascendant empire of the day. The nineteenth-century staple economy, with its industrial structure in central Canada and its wheat economy in the west, had corresponded well with a world in which Britain was still a prime economic power. The new staples of minerals and electricity, natural gas and oil, and a much-enlarged branch-plant industrial sector corresponded to a world in which the United States was emerging as *the* capitalist power par excellence, and the single most powerful state overall.

So we severed old ties with Great Britain in the post–World War II period, and established new ones with the United States. We adopted a Canadian Citizenship Act in 1947 (no longer would we simply be *British* subjects); we abolished appeals to the Judicial Committee of the Privy Council in 1949; we began to appoint Canadian-born governors general in 1952 and to drop all references to the term dominion (too colonial a ring to it).

By the 1960s we had shed the red ensign with its Union Jack in favour of the maple leaf flag; by the early 1980s we had patriated the Canadian constitution, leaving the monarchy and Commonwealth as our last vestigial ties with Britain.

With the United States we became junior partners in defence matters. This policy began with the Permanent Joint Board of Defence Canada–United States, set up in 1940 at a moment of great peril on the European front. It carried on with the Hyde Park Agreement of 1941 for collaboration in defence production, the 1947 agreement on radar lines in northern Canada, the building of the Pinetree, Mid-Canada, and DEW Lines of the early 1950s, the North American Air Defence Agreement of 1957, and the Defence Sharing Agreement of 1959.

In foreign policy, we tended to align ourselves closely on American positions in the Cold War. This explains our enthusiastic support for the creation of NATO, our participation in the Korean War, our twenty-year refusal to recognize the People's Republic of China, and our role on the International Control Commission in Indo-China. In the economic realm, American capital inflows into Canada were massive and brought a degree of American ownership of the Canadian economy by the 1950s and 1960s unmatched in any other advanced industrial state. As for popular culture, magazines, films, TV programs, and much else bore a powerful American stamp.

The other side of the coin, however, even in the heyday of American hegemony, was resistance to American control in a number of areas. This was most conspicuous in the field of culture, beginning with the creation of the Canadian Broadcasting Corporation as an alternative to the American radio networks in the 1930s. In the words of Graham Spry, founder of the League for Public Broadcasting, the choice for Canada was "the state or the States." That same stark choice led to the creation of the National Film Board during World War II, to the establishment of the Massey Royal Commission on National Development in the Arts, Letters and Sciences in 1949, and, following its recommendations, of the Canada Council in 1957. It also provided the rationale for a much-increased postwar role for the federal government in the funding of post-secondary education and research.

Something of the same imperative was at work in the establishment of Trans-Canada Airlines (later Air Canada) in 1937, of Atomic Energy of Canada Ltd during World War II, in the drive to have a gas pipeline built between Alberta and Ontario in the mid-1950s, in the creation of the National Energy Board in 1958. It surfaced in the concerns over the degree of American economic influence in Canada expressed in the Preliminary Report of the Royal Commission on Canada's Economic Prospects in 1956 and by the governor of the Bank of Canada, James Coyne, a few years later. And occasionally, as in our policy towards Cuba after 1959, Canada showed itself capable of independence from the United States.

The upsurge of a more independent-minded Canadian nationalism would not come until the late 1960s, some years after your own nationalism in Quebec had taken off. To those two developments I want to turn in my next two letters. Before I break off today, let me reiterate two main points. First, in its own way, English Canada has forged an identity based upon strong identification with the institutions of the federal state. Second, English Canada, throughout its history, has experienced simultaneous attraction to and fear of the United States. Yet the desire not to be overwhelmed has been persistent and it fuels national sentiment today. If you wish to understand us, never underestimate the two.

– III –

How the plot thickens. What began with an innocent enough attempt to explain English Canada to a Québécois friend after the election now takes on new dimensions as Canada finds itself plunged into a full-scale constitutional crisis. The Bourassa government, its ear to the ground, knowing how badly it was burnt by the language question in 1976, decides to limit the application of "freedom of expression" for English to inside signs. It invokes the notwithstanding clause both against the Canadian Charter of Rights and Freedoms and Quebec's own Charter of Rights. In Manitoba, as a direct tit-for-tat, the Conservative premier pulls the plug on the Meech Lake Accord, already threatened by the Liberal and New Democratic Party opposition in the aftermath of 21 November. Anglophone ministers resign from the Quebec government; francophone ministers vow no further constitutional discussion if Meech goes down. A classical Canadian imbroglio in the best tradition of the 1960s and 1970s.

I had intended in today's letter to evoke that period when a new Quebec consciousness came into its own, provoking in tandem a certain *prise de conscience* in English Canada. But already our parallel, and dramatically opposite, reaction to the language question round three (or is it thirteen?) suggests that nothing is new under the sun, that the battles of Saint-Léonard and Bill 22 live again.

Before I can turn to familiar themes from the recent past, let me record my impressions of the current impasse. It comes as no astonishment to one who spent the year 1987–88 in Montreal, frequenting francophone milieux in which 101 lapel pins were de rigueur, listening to conversations in which the symbolism of signs had become a question of cardinal dignity to make up for two centuries of anglophone domination, to witness from afar the outpouring of emotion at the Paul-Sauvé Arena the other night. I can put myself in your shoes, think back to what Montreal looked like in the 1950s or early 1960s with its largely English-language downtown district, and appreciate your fervour. A singular desire to right the historical English-French division of labour and language once and for all in favour of the majority is at work. And if the Anglos in Quebec must undergo the humiliation (as they and their columnists and d'Iberville Fortier, Canada's language commissioner, see it) of seeing their language excluded from public display on outside signs and the judgment of the Supreme Court overridden, *tant pis*. It is about time they learned who was master in their own house, and who, at best, a tolerated guest.

In your reactions I see also something of the same indifference to English Canada that I detected in your attitude to free trade. "What difference does it make if the whole laboriously constructed edifice of bilingualism and biculturalism comes crashing down, if the backlash against Quebec's actions leads to a lead poisoning of the atmosphere between the two societies? If English Canadians outside Quebec suddenly become concerned about their poor cousins inside Quebec, where was their concern when French Canadians were the victims? If they don't accept our right to take measures for collective self-defence (even if this infringes on certain ostensibly sacrosanct individual rights of expression), then we don't need their noble sentiments on bilingual institutions. Why need we justify our attitudes to them when it is we, and we alone, whose fate is at stake in the choice of linguistic politics for Quebec?"

To these arguments, *cher ami*, I can only answer that you owe your fellow citizens of long standing the same explanation which enlightened Frenchmen or Americans of the eighteenth century were prepared to give the world for their actions – in other words, reasoned arguments for your positions. And you have an obligation to listen to reasoned counter-arguments, on the grounds that your own case will better stand the test of public opinion if it has survived such scrutiny.

The principal counter-argument is one drawn from common folk wisdom: "One wrong does not justify another." There is no denying a long history of Québécois receiving the short end of the stick, of being born *pour un petit pain*, with relatively inferior political and economic status within Canadian society. True, you may have had your own elites – political, ecclesiastical, professional – to blame for some of this, but it does not sweeten the pill. So it was only right that beginning in 1960 you should have sought to redress the situation, using the levers of the provincial state. You took steps to modernize your educational system, to promote francophone economic activity and enterprises, to provide more significant social services to your citizens, to enhance Quebec's external presence and ties with the larger francophone world. This led to inevitable tensions with Ottawa – educational conferences in Gabon and "Vive le Québec libre" – but it was also part of a modernizing process whose results are all around you today.

You also sought to limit the attraction of English for immigrants coming to Quebec, and perhaps even for some francophones tempted to cross the linguistic line within Quebec. Riots flared in suburbs of Montreal, demands for the protection of French grew, culminating as we all know with the passage of Bill 101, the *Charte de la langue française*, in 1977. This ensured the primacy of French, not only within all governmental institutions and services, but in the larger commercial and economic life of the province (to the degree, at least, that this was not integrated into a larger Canadian and North American context). By streaming new immigrants into the French-language educational system, it set the stage for a more multi-ethnic francophone society in the future, and for a steady decline in the size of the English-language community and its institutions.

Up until this point I was prepared to support you. And I think it is fair to say that most of those on the left of the political spectrum or of a fairly liberal-minded outlook would have taken the same position. Why should one deny legitimate rights to a linguistic and cultural community to preserve itself against possible assimilation within a larger English-speaking sea? Why, to go one step further, in a world of newly independent states, deny the political right to self-determination to a people who might seek to express it? Hence, the willingness of a small handful in English Canada (I was one of them) to support the "Yes" side in the 1980 referendum, and the support of a large majority of English Canadians, despite their own emotional opposition to Quebec independence, for the right of the people of Quebec to decide democratically whether or not they wished to remain within the Canadian Confederation.

That decision, as we know, went against sovereignty-association, not least because francophone Québécois were themselves about equally divided on this option. The referendum defeat triggered a subsequent round of constitutional negotiations, culminating in the Charter of Rights and the patriation formula of November 1981 which the Quebec government refused to endorse. It also indirectly set the stage for a second round of constitutional negotiations, resulting in the 1987 Meech Lake Accord, which further reaffirmed the specificity of Quebec. And until 21 November 1988 I was prepared to swallow hard, despite real fears about the weakening of federal authority, and accept Meech Lake for precisely this reason.

The hard question I have for you today is whether your continued survival really rests on imposing Bill 101 to the letter, with only the most innocuous of amendments. Is it really worth jettisoning the latest Supreme Court judgment, making light of the minority position of anglophones within Quebec society, the better to assert the rights of the majority? What price majority rights, collective national rights versus individual, or, if one prefers, versus the collective rights of a national minority? Can the identity of one group only flourish if that of the other is denied?

Correct me if I am wrong, *cher ami*, but I detect a simple desire for vengeance, for paying the Anglos back for their sins of omission and commission, in your current outpouring of emotion. And forgive me if I refuse to go along this time, not finding in such a motive sufficient justification for your actions. Would some bilingual signs in the Montreal districts of NDG or Snowdon with English lettering significantly smaller than the French really bring the edifice of French culture in Quebec crumbling down? Would the offer of some tacit recognition of the legitimacy of the language of the shrinking anglophone minority not suggest a maturing of Quebec nationalism, an ability at last to extend a hand to that minority whose role may have been most problematic in your history, but which has made valiant efforts in recent years to accommodate itself to the new Quebec? And would not this gesture, at the same time, represent a symbolic acknowledgment to English Canada that its acceptance of bilingualism and biculturalism as a permanent part of the Canadian identity has not gone unnoticed?

I know how difficult it is for old antagonists (not to speak of enemies) to extend recognition (and with it forgiveness) to one another. One thinks of the many steps that Israelis and Palestinians will have to take until this has been achieved. One knows how much further away yet is reconciliation between Afrikaaners and whites on the one hand, South African blacks and coloureds on the other. We know of the fearful blood hatreds at work in Sri Lanka, the Lebanon or northern Ireland and have reasons to wonder whether reconciliation will ever be achieved.

Perhaps I am a hopeless dreamer, like Joseph in the Old Testament. Perhaps a fancier of utopian schemes. Yet in my naiveté I believe it is possible, nay necessary, to reach out a hand of friendship, even to one's adversary, to not hold grudges forever, to be prepared to see the world, if only in part, through the eyes of the other. The ultimate justification for nationalism, I am convinced, is that one see not only one's own interests and how they may be threatened or enhanced, but also those of the other with whom one has been thrown together. It is because you have not heeded this principle that I find your reaction to the Supreme Court ruling so difficult to accept.

The same lament infuses my reaction to your nationalism of recent years, to your vote of 21 November. You have simply become too selfish, interested only in *your* fate, *your* interests, supremely indifferent to those of that other linguistic and cultural community that makes up Canada. And selfishness, *cher ami*, by the standards of eighteenth-century enlightenment or twentieth-century moral and political philosophy is *not* a base on which to build a good society.

Heaven knows, we in English Canada are also capable of egoism and indifference. I am not holding us up as paragons of virtue. Yet there has been an increased responsiveness to Quebec and its demands since the Quiet Revolution, an openness, of which the willingness to accept the results of the 1980 referendum without flinching is a perfect example (Can one imagine India permitting such a referendum to be held in the Punjab, Iraq in its Kurdish provinces, Yugoslavia in Kosovo?), a tolerance and sense of fair play that are not to be spurned. For all our faults, we have not scorned you, turned our backs on you, or refused to recognize in you something more than a sometime rival – a blood relation. And foolishly perhaps, but probably justly, we have expected you to respond in kind.

Voilà – my reactions to the events of recent days. Do not take the easy way out, filing these letters away as the hue and cry of an outsider, *un étranger*, who refuses to understand. Listen, for once, to the words of a friend who would listen to yours, and accept that you have no more claim to a monopoly on virtue and truth than he has. And that even your heartfelt linguistic concerns must not become absolutes that efface the "other's" claim to some stake in the homeland you call Quebec and that we persist in calling Canada.

IV

It is time to explore a little more closely the roots of our twin nationalisms in recent decades. We live in a world that is becoming more integrated, more internationalized, more corrosive of sovereignty in its traditional nineteenth-century form. From youth culture to yuppies, from fashions to films, we are far more influenced by currents that cut across the advanced capitalist countries than by purely internal developments. For a period, both in Canada and Europe, it was fashionable to refer to this as Americanization; we are now conscious that, much as with capitalism, we are talking about technological and cultural forces that are global.

Simultaneously, however, and this is one of the paradoxes of the late twentieth century, national differences persist, and certain forms of nationalism have even increased in importance. This has been especially true of nationalism linked to language, and to groups within long-established nation states which have felt themselves to be in an inferior position, politically, economically, or culturally. Examples drawn from the developed countries would include the Basques and the Catalans, the Bretons and the Corsicans, the Scots and the Welsh, the Walloons and the Flemish, and the Québécois. Linguistic and cultural nationalism can flare up when a group feels its advance throttled or its existing status no longer commensurate with what it takes to be its real place in the world. It can be associated with social classes – entrepreneurial ones, professionals and the middle class, the working class – or various combinations of these. It may be influenced by developments in the world at large, for example the achievement of independence by scores of former European colonies in the decades following World War II. It may also be influenced by more general social or ideological forces – radical contesting of existing authority in the 1960s, the turn to more conservative or market-driven values by the 1980s.

It is my contention, *cher ami*, that your nationalism cannot be understood without reference to some of these larger forces. This is not to deny you specific concerns, or to abstract from one's analysis events as varied as Maurice Duplessis's death in September 1959 or Charles de Gaulle's 1967 visit, the personalities of René Lévesque or Pierre Trudeau, the challenges of modernizing a society which had lagged behind Canadian and North American norms in a number of telling respects. We must not, however, fall into the trap that I fear most of your intellectuals have fallen into, of treating Quebec as some type of closed society with its own unique laws of development. (To be fair, I will also admit that a certain number of English Canadian historians, social scientists and cultural critics commit exactly the same error with regard to English Canada.)

When I think back to the Quebec of the 1960s and 1970s, certain things stand out. One is the remarkable sense of new possibilities, new ways of thinking and acting, which would have been impossible in the traditional Quebec of which Duplessis had become a maleficent symbol. There was a thaw in Quebec society, much as in the Soviet Union following Stalin's death, or in the Gorbachev years with a whole generation of both young and middle-aged able to throw off the shackles of received orthodoxy in one fell swoop. In Quebec, of course, it was clerical authority and retrograde notions of the role of the state which were swept aside in the first years of the Quiet Revolution. Reforms were undertaken – the creation of a merit-based civil service, of a more secular educational system, of interventionist economic policies, of an industrial relations systems offering greater legitimacy to trade unions, of a more comprehensive network of state-run social services from hospitals to pensions.

What was happening in society at large was no less important. The language of radical decolonization – of Memmi, Sartre, or Fanon – was becoming fashionable among the student young, the readers of *Le Quartier Latin* or *Parti pris*. Students were demonstrating against the anti-French stance of the president of the CNR, Donald Gordon, but also in support of civil rights in the United States and against the war in Vietnam. The first bombs of the Front de Libération du Québec went off in 1963, and for the next seven years analogies with the IRA or ETA in Spain seemed perfectly in order. At the same time, labour, flexing its muscles and greatly strengthened by unionization in the public sector, would increasingly confront both private capital and the state in a crescendo of contestation of which the 1971 strike at *La Presse* and the 1972 Common Front strike were the high points.

It has become something of a *cliché* now to analyse the Quiet Revolution in terms of the emergence of a new middle class. And who could deny the appearance of university-trained francophones in significant numbers within an expanded civil service, in middle and senior management positions within newly expanded state enterprises like Hydro-Québec, or in educational institutions? When one thinks of the traditional French Canadian political and social elite – notaries and lawyers, small town businessmen, the clergy – of the low French Canadian participation rates in education compared to English Canadians, or of their remarkable underrepresentation in what one might call the commanding heights of the economy, then the changes inaugurated in 1960 were indeed dramatic.

Here language served the interests of class and vice versa. The new middle classes were no longer prepared to accept English domination of the economic levers of society, and would use the state as a powerful instrument to promote a larger francophone presence. The state and para-state sector would provide thousands of jobs for the university-trained, and pressure private sector employers to increase the number of francophone employees. And the federal government, sensitive to rising national concerns in Quebec, would create many openings in its rush to make the federal civil service bilingual.

The new middle class was paramount in the language battles of the period. They provided the backbone for the Rassemblement pour l'Indépendance nationale (RIN) and subsequently the Parti Québécois. They marched for a French McGill and for tough laws which would make French the official language of Quebec and steer future immigrants into francophone educational institutions. They took umbrage at any constitutional changes (the 1964 Fulton-Favreau proposals, the 1971 Victoria formula) that would not recognize Quebec's special status, and strongly favoured attempts to promote Quebec's position internationally. If for some the French Revolution has been seen as bourgeois and the Soviet as proletarian, then the Quiet Revolution might be seen as that of the new middle class.

The main problem with such an analysis is that it makes light of the group that was to prove the main beneficiary of this new nationalism – the francophone bourgeoisie or capitalist class. It is all very well to highlight the enhanced position of artists or intellectuals during those years of ferment – it is flattering to those in the cultural or academic domain to see themselves occupying centre stage. It is certainly true that the state sector grew dramatically during this period, as indeed it did in the English-speaking provinces, for the 1960s – the decade of the real coming of the welfare state to Canada with medicare, the Canada Pension Plan, and revamped social assistance programs – also brought significant increases in state expenditure there. Under the surface, what was being promoted in Quebec was something other than Gilles Vigneault or Pauline Julien, *marxisant* periodicals or publishing houses. The long-term goal of state economic ventures like Hydro-Québec, the Société Générale de financement, or the Caisse de dépôt was the promotion of a Québécois-based capitalism in which francophone entre-preneurs would finally come into their own. If one studies the period with care and reads the statements of Jean Lesage or René Lévesque or Jacques Parizeau or Robert Bourassa, one discovers that the real name of the game is the creation of Quebec en-terprises able to compete with those of their anglophone ho-mologues.

An important component of linguistic nationalism was the opening of corporate doors to greater francophone participa-tion. A direct effect of the challenge to the entrenched position of English, and of the significant flight of middle- and upper-class anglophones after the PQ's electoral victory and the intro-duction of Bill 101, was new openings for francophones at the pinnacle of Quebec's economic institutions. By the 1980s, Bom-bardier and Lavalin, Provigo and Laurentien had become the symbols of a new entrepreneurial Quebec, of that society's acces-sion to capitalist modernity, after 150 years of relative back-wardness.

It is remarkable how little this emerging capitalist ethos figures in the intellectual writings of the 1960s. These often pointed in a radically different direction, towards collectivism or socialism, goals that I must admit most attracted me to Quebec nationalism twenty-five years ago. For I had become politicized in the Montreal of the early 1960s (at McGill, if one dares men-tion the name), a period in which students around the world were beginning to turn to the left, after a long postwar calm in the West in which anti-communism had been the prevailing ideology. Among francophones in Quebec, for the first time in your history, socialist ideas, powerfully imbued with nationalism, would enjoy real favour, where previously they had been ruth-lessly rooted out by conservative and clerical orthodoxy. Im-perialism, class struggle, bourgeoisie, popular movements, working class were terms that suddenly became part of the vocabulary of the young. Analogies were made to the struggles in Algeria or the American South, in the desire to fuse class with national liberation. Quebec's "white niggers of America" seemed one of the weak links in the larger imperialist chain that could yet be broken as popular energies were mobilized.

As I think back to that period, I am aware of just how much illusion your left laboured under. Yet in a period which saw student occupations at Berkeley or Columbia and mass rallies against the Vietnam War, a radical student movement in those recently defeated World War II belligerents, Japan and West Germany, a Gaullist regime rocked to its foundations by a student revolt in May 1968, anything seemed possible. So why not *terre Québec* as a haven of socialist liberation, after the long night of obscurantism and colonial repression?

Some were prepared to play the armed vanguard in hastening that moment along. Such was the role of the FLQ, believing that bombings and kidnappings – "the revolution of the deed" – would lift the veil from the masses and spark their revolt. Others turned to the trade unions, infusing them with a degree of radical language (one thinks of the trade union manifestos of the early 1970s) without parallel in English Canada. And still others turned to organizing movements for day care, tenants' rights, immigrants, women, all of which collectively pointed the way to an alternative Quebec.

It is easy today to grow cynical about much of this, knowing how quickly grand projects dissolve into dust. The Marxist-Leninist language adopted by some of the groups (En Lutte, La Ligue communiste) proved quite alien to ordinary Quebec workers, welfare recipients, or immigrants, while their dogmatic tendencies hastened their own demise. The trade union movement, for all its radicalism, was not really seeking the revolutionary transformation of society or the overthrow of capitalism, as became evident in the aftermath of the 1972 Common Front strike. And various activists and intellectuals of the left quickly went on to occupy respectable niches within society – in the universities, the media, the PQ, or the civil service.

As in France, where the dreams of the *soixante-huitards* – the students of May 1968 – gave way to the sober reality of Pompidou, Giscard, and even Mitterrand, or in America where the anti-war movement spawned Richard Nixon and eventually Ronald Reagan, so in Quebec the radical left proved but a marginal actor. The PQ's nine years in power were to see the enactment of the tough language laws for which the new middle class had pressed. And, in its first years of office, it passed a fairly progressive labour code, making Quebec, for example, the only jurisdiction in North America that outlaws scabs. Yet, with the economic downturn of the early 1980s, the PQ government had become as restraint-oriented as governments of the right, rolling back public sector wages in the years 1982–83, and abandoning any illusions of grand social reform. By the mid-1980s, the political options in Quebec had become little other than a choice between two parties for whom the logic of the marketplace and the promotion of francophone entrepreneurs was the prevailing one.

Cher ami, I do not mean to castigate you because your left has so lamentably failed; that of English Canada has also fallen on hard times in the 1980s. Nor do I want to make light of the real changes for the good that came out of the two decades following 1960 – the establishment of a welfare state in Quebec, a more Keynesian thrust to public policy, a larger role for public sector institutions, a climate more favourable to labour and popular institutions than before. These are not mean achievements, and along with a new sense of national pride and linguistic and cultural affirmation have become hallmarks of a permanently transformed Quebec. I simply wish to remind you that the assumption that nationalism would usher in some form of socialism was gravely mistaken; on the contrary, nationalist argument had much more to do with the emergence of a new Quebec capitalist class, *les nouveaux guerriers* as they have sometimes been called. And there is no class more hostile to policies of redistribution or egalitarian principles than this one.

I shall go on to argue in my next letter that we in English Canada who called ourselves nationalists in the 1960s and 1970s may also have helped create a stronger Canadian capitalist class fundamentally hostile to the values of the left. We may have been your *compagnons de route* in fooling ourselves about the real possibilities and limits to social change in our part of North America. Like you, we helped create a new nationalism and have been marked by it. Like you, we find ourselves searching for better alternatives in a neo-conservative era.

Yet our starting points may differ in terms of our loyalties and sense of community. And it is this, more even than the international restructuring of capital now underway, that stands in the way of a more progressive politics in the Canada of to-morrow.

V

It is time to talk about English Canada and its nationalism since 1960. I know that to you this is terra incognita, that you imagine it to be the invention of a few Toronto intellectuals jealous of their Quebec *confrères* and trying to persuade a largely apathetic population that English Canada too is a vibrant place, with a sense of identity to match Quebec's. Good cynic that you are, you dismiss such "fabrications" out of hand, convinced that, like their forefathers, English Canadians are a nation of shopkeepers with the bank ledger as their overriding concern.

Even a nation of shopkeepers, however, as both Britain and Canada were to prove in two world wars, is prepared to bleed profusely when it feels national interests are at stake. (Surely you remember how bitterly French Canadians rejected the pro-British nationalism of English Canadians during those two conflicts!) Nor has the Britain of Margaret Thatcher at the time of the Falklands crisis, or for that matter the United States of the post-war era (another nation of shopkeepers, or more correctly, multinational corporations), exactly disdained nationalism. So it is necessary to be less supercilious towards English Canadians, who are also capable of strong national feeling.

There is one important difference, I will grant you, between your nationalism and ours. Ours does not have the linguistic component of yours, nor do we feel ourselves to be a minority people within this country in the way that you do (whatever our inferiority complex vis-à-vis the United States). This is significant psychologically, and has tended to make English Canadians less defensive overall about their nationalism and less fearful of disappearing down a historical black holes. Yet this difference is one of degree, rather than of kind.

As I began to explain in letter II, there has always been a love-hate relationship between English Canada and the United States. The cultural attraction has been strong, the economic integration powerful, and the populations, because of geographical proximity and shared language, given to a good deal of intermingling. It has been difficult to whip up feelings that the United States is an enemy – the *hostis* familiar to certain theories of international relations. Still, the "unarmed border" has posed threats of a different sort, and the sheer size of the United States – a ratio of population and wealth of 10 to 1 to Canada and 12 to 1 to English Canada – sufficient to give many of us pause.

In the 1960s, in particular, English Canada was to go through a wrenching reappraisal of our relations with the United States. We had long since shed our British tropism, and suddenly began to wonder about the American one that had taken its place. There were good reasons for these doubts: the resistance to civil rights in the American South; evidence that American power deployed around the world was in the service, not of freedom, but of puppet regimes and its own great power interests; concern that the costs of American ownership in our manufacturing and resource sectors outweighed the benefits. There was the turn to a more assertive Canadianism, fostered, in part, by events such as Canada's Centennial and by a perceived weakening in American postwar hegemony.

Foreign ownership was the focus of several government reports (the 1968 Watkins Report, the 1970 Wahn Report, Herb Gray's 1972 Task Force report), and a key concern both of the Waffle movement within the NDP and the Committee for an Independent Canada. The latter, in particular, with a claimed membership of 200,000 at its height, and such prestigious figures as Walter Gordon on its steering committee, sought governmental policies which would promote Canadian control – both public and private – over the economy, thereby significantly reducing the American stake. It was English Canada's version of *Maîtres chez nous*, and its instruments would be the Canadian Development Corporation (CDC) and the Foreign Investment Review Agency (FIRA), established in the early 1970s.

A corollary demanded in various quarters was for a foreign policy based on something other than junior partnership with the United States. Lester Pearson in 1965 had sensed the change in direction, when he had called, in a speech in Philadelphia, for a halt to the US bombing of North Vietnam. Yet that same year, the Merchant-Heeney Report written by two senior Canadian and American diplomats had sanctioned "quiet diplomacy" as the best course for US-Canada relations. The pressures for disengaging Canada from the American empire grew with calls for the withdrawal of Canadian troops stationed in Germany, for an end to the NORAD alliance, for the recognition of the People's Republic of China, and for a more independent Canadian stance in the world at large. Some of these changes were to be carried out during the Trudeau period, with an emphasis after 1971 on a so-called third option to Canadian foreign policy, seeking through ties with Europe, Japan, and the third world some diversification from our links to the United States. Though little ultimately came of all this, it does stand in stark contrast to the cravenly pro-American tilt of the Mulroney government.

In the cultural field, the 1970s were to see the ending of tax exemptions on advertising in the Canadian editions of magazines like *Time* and *Reader's Digest*, and a set of policies to encourage filmmakers, book publishers, and arts groups of various sorts. More significantly, from my point of view, Canadian literature, theatre, dance, and music came of age, not unlike what Quebec had experienced in the 1960s. There were new audiences for all these forms of cultural expression, and, within our universities, pressures for greater Canadian content in the humanities and social sciences.

The irony from your point of view, no doubt, is that this stronger Canadian nationalism came to be associated with a government headed by a man who for many of you was *the* enemy of Quebec nationalism, Pierre Trudeau. The fostering of a greater Canadian nationalism might be seen by some as a conscious effort on his part to build up the Canadian state as a counterweight to Quebec's, to promote pan-Canadian federal symbols pleasing to English Canadian nationalists, but not to French Canadian. Moreover, the proponent of third options in foreign policy or the Foreign Investment Review Act was the man who had invoked the War Measures Act in October 1970, a measure which hard nationalists saw as directed against Quebec.

Things are not quite so simple, as I now see in retrospect. I was a graduate student in Toronto at the time of the October crisis, and recall the futile attempts by small groups of those on the left to speak out against the War Measures Act and what we saw as "the occupation of Quebec." We felt strongly for the 450 who had been arrested unjustly in Quebec, for the suspension of civil liberties, and for the deliberate escalation of the crisis through the federal government's recourse to emergency powers. Yet I remember that close to 90 per cent of Canadians – both English- and French-speaking, according to polls at the time – supported the actions of the federal government, and that legitimacy remained overwhelmingly on the side of constituted authority, not of the FLQ. Nor did Quebec nationalism really suffer the mortal blow in October 1970 that some had feared. True, the route of armed insurrection and urban guerrila movements seemed permanently barred thereafter. But the PQ was to receive increased support in the following years, coming to power in November 1976 and, despite the referendum defeat, remaining in power until December 1985.

It would be wrong, moreover, to see the new nationalism of English Canada as embodied primarily in Pierre Trudeau.

Many of the governmental measures introduced during his years in office – the CDC or FIRA – were done under strong pressure from the nationalist wing of his own party or from the NDP, when it held the balance of power between 1972 and 1974. Trudeau, in words if not always in deeds, was no fonder of the nationalism of English Canada than of that of Quebec. The social forces pushing for a more independent Canadian position vis-à-vis the United States, for a more interventionist role by the federal government in carrying this out, were not worlds apart from those that had played so important a role during your Quiet Revolution.

We had our new middle class coming into its own – academics, teachers, scientists, professionals, students, civil servants – whose increased political activism and nationalism coincided with an increased role for the state generally. Some of these, like the student movement or the Waffle, were inclined in a strongly leftwards direction; others in a more mainstream, albeit interventionist one. All found in Canadian nationalism a common cause. For some, this might be a concern to make Canadian universities less beholden to American teaching staff and disciplinary models; for others, a desire for greater funding of research and development; for still others, the search for enhanced Canadian independence in the energy or resource sector, of which Petro-Canada or provincial crown corporations like the Potash Corporation of Saskatchewan became the symbols.

The trade union movement, too, would gradually take on a more Canadian complexion. In the early 1960s, the Canadian Labour Congress (CLC) was largely made up of the affiliates of American unions, many of whom had only marginal autonomy in the running of their own affairs. We had no Confederation of National Trade Unions (CNTU), entirely Quebec-based, which formed the backbone of a more left-oriented unionism in your society. But we, like you, experienced a significant wave of public sector unionism in the 1960s, which created strong Canadian counterparts like the Canadian Union of Public Employees or the Public Sector Alliance of Canada to the international unions. The pressure also existed for unions like the Steelworkers and the Autoworkers to accord their Canadian affiliates greater autonomy than before. Eventually, unions like the Canadian Pulpworkers and the Canadian Autoworkers were to go it entirely alone, severing their connection with the American unions. Today, less than 40 per cent of the membership of the CLC is affiliated to the so-called internationals, compared to over 70 per cent in the early 1960s.

What our nationalists, especially those of the left, failed to realize were the very real interests which would continue to bind Canadian to American capital, albeit in new ways. Overall, big businesses, such as banks, industrial corporations, resource producers, were not supporters of the new nationalism in the late 1960s and 1970s. Some had already succeeded in going multinational; others hoped to go the same route; and the majority had grown accustomed to close ties with American branch plants located in this country.

There was also a regional component to their response, with capital in the resource sectors, particularly outside central Canada, generally hostile to nationalist moves by the federal government. Quebec did not have the monopoly on regional loyalties and province-building. Alberta could play a similar game, and could with time find its government pitted no less strongly against Ottawa. This came to a head with the National Energy Program in 1980–81, when the federal government increased its take on royalties from oil and gas producers in the west to help finance its Canadianization policies. In retaliation, Alberta threatened to cut back the rate of production at the wellhead. Simultaneously, western separatism began to gain support.

This, incidentally, underlines a further difference between English Canadian nationalism and yours. Ours must come to terms with regional complexities, stemming from real differences in regional political economies. It is not only Quebec that sustains the federal-provincial division of labour in Canada. The othe provinces also have interests which can conflict with those of Ottawa and which, in the case of the western provinces, have frequently led to such clashes. (Aberhardt and Social Credit in Alberta, W.A.C. Bennett and the Columbia River Treaty, the NDP and potash nationalization in Saskatchewan, Peter Lougheed and the National Energy Program). We would be no more unitary a state were Quebec to leave Confederation. At most, the differences between our regions would be less coloured by linguistic and cultural factors.

Let me return to my major argument regarding the attitudes of big business towards Canadian nationalism. To put things in a nutshell, I would contend that its members were simultaneously nationalism's chief critics and chief beneficiaries. For all its disdain for FIRA or the CDC, Canadian big business saw its relative strength within the Canadian economy, measured by assets, profits, or sales, increase simultaneously. The period witnessed a maturing of Canadian capitalism, with American control over the manufacturing and resource sectors declining to well under 50 per cent of the total, and with Canadian investment in the United States increasing at a far greater rate than American in Canada. (Canadian investment in the United States amounted to some 15 per cent of the value of American in Canada in the early 1960s, and had grown to close to 50 per cent of the value of American capital in Canada by the early 1980s.) Much like your new capitalists, it was our Norandas and Olympia and Yorks and Northern Telecoms and major banks that had grown exponentially while Canadian nationalism had held sway. And it was these same interests that were to come out most forcefully in support of free trade with the United States in the 1980s, backing it through thick and thin in the 1988 election.

More on the politics of free trade in a future letter. Let me conclude this one with the following observations. First, Canadian nationalism in the 1960s and 1970s was new, because it was neither pro-British nor pro-American, but strictly Canadian in orientation. Second, it tended to look to a strong role for the federal state (and for provincial governments) in promoting a greater degree of Canadian ownership and control over the economy, and to cultural and external policies to match these. Third, it was, much like Quebec nationalism of the same period, strongly rooted in the new middle class, though it also won support from Canadian labour and, here and there, from business. Overall, big business was hostile to economic nationalism and has remained so to this day. Fourth, there were regional components to English Canada and its political economy that, in varying degrees, undercut the competitive appeal of nationalism. Fifth, the new Canadian nationalism was in no way opposed to Quebec's self-affirmation as symbolized by the Quiet Revolution, or to legitimate measures to promote Quebec's linguistic and cultural specificity. Many English Canadians were prepared to embrace bilingualism and biculturalism as a set of policies for the whole of Canada, where an earlier Canadian nationalism would have balked. Some, like supporters of the Waffle, were prepared to recognize Quebec's right to self-determination, up to and including independence. In exchange, however, English Canadian nationalists hoped and expected that Quebec nationalists would share their own concerns about Canada's (and Quebec's) excessive integration with the United States. On this last point, 21 November 1988 was to demonstrate how mistaken they had been.

VI

Cher ami, I find it difficult to keep up this correspondence. I want to gesture, to see your facial expressions, as though we were seated in a café on Laurier or Saint-Denis, with the evening before us. I want to hear back from you, more than the predictable responses and scornful put-downs I find myself forced to invent. I recognize the tyranny of distance that separates us at opposite ends of this country. Geographical spaces are large, too large to overcome easily the further divide that language and collective sentiments instil. Perhaps it was a delusion, despite railways and airlines and telecommunication networks, to attempt to weave a country out of such disparate elements.

Only when we go overseas do some of these differences begin to dissolve. I remember my experiences in Paris in the late 1960s, at the Maison du Canada, where suddenly English Canadians and Québécois, thrown into this fascinating but unfamiliar maelstrom called France, found themselves feeling North American together vis-à-vis the French. It was not a matter of forgetting all our differences; this was precisely the decade when nationalist fervour was running strongest in Quebec and beginning to surface in English Canada. But it was perfectly clear to you that you were not French, could never be French, for all the ostensible bonds that language and ethnic origin provided. One could be fascinated by philosophical and sociological discourse, by theatre and films, restaurants and cafés, one could read one's *Le Monde* and attend seminars at the École pratique des hautes études to one's heart's content, and never cross that invisible line. Anglophones like me could meet with you and speak with you on a daily basis, knowing that Paris provided the neutral territory in which our two solitudes could interact.

Friendships were formed that have lasted to this day; inhibitions were overcome that in Montreal would have been impossible to surmount, the cosmopolitanism of the city and its extraordinary university milieu making our petty national differences pale by comparison. Those who were on the left were on the left regardless of whether they were anglophone or francophone, Greek or Turk, Brazilian or Argentinian. Those who sought to crack the riddles of structuralism or critical theory, semiotics or theatre of the absurd, were thrown together pell-mell in their common concerns. We were citizens of something larger than Canada or Quebec, though we had not lost our moorings in our respective societies.

I evoke this period with a certain nostalgia, not because it seems so much more difficult to recreate the same type of feeling on the shores of the St Laurence, Lake Ontario, or English Bay. No, my nostalgia is for those years when one was twenty or twenty-five and everything, for one brief moment, seemed possible. It is for those walks through the Parc Montsouris or the Jardin de Luxembourg, those all-night vigils to the muses of poetry, eros and revolution, those amphitheatres from which the old mole of revolution might, at any moment, poke its head. It was the sixties, when to be young was to reject authority, conventional wisdom, and the dull routines that an organized capitalism (and state socialism) secreted from every pore.

I know nothing is gained from romanticizing this fading past. The student left lived with its own illusions, far removed from the day-to-day concerns of ordinary citizens. The long period of postwar prosperity had about run its course, and harder times, meaner times, were ahead for the western world. Participatory democracy (*Élections = trahison*), the imagination in power, a more worker-controlled economy proved impossible ideals to sustain when the magic moment of barricades in the

Latin Quarter or heated discussion in universities under siege had passed. We would have to get on with our lives as best we could, within Max Weber's iron cage ("With the rise of bureaucracy, the magic disappears from the world").

What, you may ask, does all this have to do with our predicament here and now, in the Quebec and Canada of the late 1980s? Nothing – and a great deal. For I write you at the end of a decade when neo-conservative ideals have cut a swath through the western world, when personal success, ambition, conformity, attainment are the prevailing ethos and market principles the sacred totems of economists, philosophers, and politicians alike. Where once Herbert Marcuse, Jean-Paul Sartre, or John Kenneth Galbraith held court, honour now goes to F.A. Hayek, Milton Friedman, Mancur Olsen, or Robert Nozick, the proponents of individual, not social, goals. Where a decade ago, Canadians might still worry about excessive corporate concentration, such as the takeover of Argus Corporation by Power, today the dominant refrain is that Canadian corporations must become larger to compete at a world scale. Where politicians a decade ago were apt to use the label "social democratic," today no politicians in power federally or provincially would do the same. We have turned to the right as a society, become more selfish overall, less interested in the promotion of collective over individual goods.

We have had particularly bitter experiences of this here in British Columbia, where a succession of Social Credit governments since 1982, faced with a downturn in the resource sector, decided to mount a major offensive against social services and organized labour. Welfare rates were slashed, tenants' rights were curtailed, the human rights commission axed, the public sector pruned drastically, education expenditures frozen, and the labour code rewritten to assist non-union employers to curb the recourse to strikes. Public services, from maintenance of provincial highways to facilities in provincial parks to gas distribution, have been privatized in the name of the nostrums of a right, such as the Fraser Institute, seeking "to get the state off our backs." The result, inevitably, has been a polarized society, in which the race is to the swiftest (or should one say the nastiest?), with the notion of community fast receding.

There have been moves in a similar direction in a number of other provinces, including Alberta, Saskatchewan, and New-foundland. And you in Quebec, since Robert Bourassa has returned to power as overseer of a new economic miracle – the flowering of Quebec entrepreneurship – have seen aspects of the same. The Commission on Privatization that reported in 1986 suggested a wholesale reversion from publicly controlled enterprises to private ones. Welfare rates have been cut back, especially for single individuals under thirty, student aid frozen, and the general tone become one in which the creation of new wealth, not a more just redistribution of existing wealth, is extolled. Still, a little more of the welfare state ethos of the 1960s and 1970s persists in the Quebec of the late 1980s than in the province from which I write.

At the federal level as well, more right-wing norms prevail. This was spelled out clearly enough in Michael Wilson's 1984 budget statement, the first after the Conservatives assumed office. The hue and cry, however, when pension cuts were in the works, subsequently stemmed the move to more full-blooded neo-conservatism, at least in social services. This has not been true of the government sector overall, where the emphasis has been on deficit reduction, reducing public sector employment, privatizing crown corporations like Air Canada and, perhaps, Petro-Canada, and on tax reform primarily of benefit to the top 10 to 20 per cent of income earners and the largest corporations.

Canada – and Quebec – have become less generous societies in their social philosophies, more market-driven than a decade or two ago. Forces of the left or liberal-left, be they trade unions, women's groups, peace groups, or church organizations, have found themselves increasingly on the defensive. It is less fashionable to challenge the consumerist values of capitalism – I write this when the Christmas shopping fever is again upon us – or the profit motive underlying it, when state socialist regimes from China to the Soviet Union to Hungary are discovering new virtues in that selfsame system. In a reversal of Mao's 1957 adage, the west wind is prevailing over the east.

We should not fool ourselves. The real heroes of our age, the ones with pictures on the covers of glossy magazines like the Globe and Mail *Report on Business Magazine* or *Actualités*, are the multimillionaires and billionaires, the authors of corporate takeover and expansion. Our politicians curry their favour, our university administrators eat out of their hands, TV programs from "Dallas" to "Venture" record their feats. The generation of 1968, Canadian or Québécois, is reduced to the middle-aged antics and escapism of Denys Arcand's film *Le déclin de l'empire américain*. The real action lies elsewhere.

Why should this bother me, you ask, as you sip a little Armagnac. Because, a trifle foolishly no doubt, I have remained faithful to the ideals of twenty years ago, to an egalitarianism that can be read back from twentieth-century social democracy to nineteenth-century Marxism, from John Stuart Mill, a trenchant critic of the inheritance of property, to Jean-Jacques Rousseau with his brilliant aperçus on the origins of inequality. It is not a matter of denouncing private property root and branch, in some late-twentieth-century version of Pierre-Joseph Proudhon's outburst that property is theft. But it is a matter of not forgetting the losers in our casino capitalism, the victims in both our own societies and around the globe. It is a matter of advancing a vision in which the privileged group in our society, our ruling economic elite, no longer exercizes the type of power over politics, the economy, or information that it does today. Rousseau was profoundly correct when he contrasted the patriotism of the simple craftsman or peasant with the values of the wealthy. "The latter belong[ed] to the land of the rich" – a land in which community, culture, and language were as nothing compared to the importance of private economic gain.

It is because this latter value prevails in post–Quiet Revolution Quebec and in an English Canada which free trade will drive ever closer to the American "free enterprise" model, that I am writing these letters. We need to remember that we live by more than bread, for more than increases in gross national product. That there are collective values – national self-realization, social justice, environmental preservation, and public liberties – that also count.

You have just been through a bout of such collectivist concern with respect to language. We have been through a moment of collective consciousness-raising with respect to free trade. Yet many in English Canada, myself included, feel profoundly hurt by your lack of concern when what we took to be our future as a nation was at stake. And you, as I have noted before, have proven supremely indifferent to questions of minority language rights or freedom of expression, obsessed as you have become with imposing the hegemony of French language and culture within Quebec. The result is a stalemate in terms of constitutional accommodation between our two societies. So let me in my next two letters address in succession the twin themes of free trade and Meech Lake.

VII

You may well wonder what the fuss has been about. The Common Market passed the thirty-year mark not so long ago, and in 1992 most of the remaining barriers to the free movement of people and capital within the European Community will disappear. Australia and New Zealand seem to have survived their free trade arrangement well enough. And in the world at large, the General Agreement on Tariffs and Trade (GATT) has led to a general lowering of tariffs and a more liberalized trading climate through the whole of the postwar period.

Why then should free trade, or more specifically the Canada–US Trade Agreement, have provoked such an outburst of emotion during the recent election campaign? Why should critics of the deal and the two opposition parties have railed against it in such apocalyptic terms, as though the survival of Canada were at stake, our every social program threatened, our natural resources even more likely to be mortgaged in the future than they had been in the past? Were we simply engaging in symbolic politics in English Canada, or were there deeper reasons for the widespread fears?

Reassure yourself, I am not about to rehash the election campaign, quoting relevant sections from the agreement, framing them within my argument, in order to persuade you of the iniquities that lie hidden from view. I propose something a little different – a discussion of the politics surrounding the trade deal, and of the social forces on both sides. I then want to say a little more about the implications of the ways in which Quebec and much of English Canada reacted to the issues and about the resulting cleavage, which the recent override of the Supreme Court judgment by the Quebec government has deepened.

A few words about the symbolism of free trade may be in order first. It is a well-known fact that throughout Canadian history the issue of free trade has been a divisive one, no more so than in 1911. In a general way, the Liberal Party was historically given to support it, and the Conservatives, beginning in 1878–79, to opposition. Western Canada was generally in favour, for the very good reason that western staple producers found themselves exporting goods to unprotected world markets and buying more expensive manufactured goods from protected eastern manufacturers. Central Canada, especially Ontario, took the opposite position.

As late as 1947–48, when postwar continentalism was in full flight, there had been secret negotiations for a free trade agreement which Prime Minister MacKenzie King, worried about nationalist backlash, had squelched. A decade later, John Diefenbaker, at the beginning of his ill-fated administration, had set out to re-orient some of Canada's trade with the United States back to Britain – to no avail. And his defeat in 1963, with the United States playing an important behind-the-scenes role, came to be interpreted by the Tory philosopher, George Grant, as the end of Canada, the triumph of technocratic liberalism and the American dream.

Grant, in fact, was premature in his lament and somewhat mistaken in his reading of who would be the major agent of our Americanization in the late twentieth century. It was his beloved Conservative Party, decreasingly Tory and increasingly business liberal, that was to be God's chosen instrument (so to speak) through which the remaining barriers to our economic integration would be overcome. Mulroney, the former president of a branch-plant operation, Iron Ore of Canada, would dare to do what Diefenbaker and, for that matter, Robert Stanfield would never have undertaken.

Grant was less wrong in pointing a finger at the business communities of both Toronto and Montreal, whom he accused of lacking even minimal loyalty to this country. There can be no doubt that the greatest impetus for further economic integration has come from precisely this quarter. Yet theirs would be a trammelled victory, for they would have to contend with the forces of a strengthened Canadian nationalism of which I wrote earlier.

Nothing could have been more at odds with free trade than the spirit of economic nationalism that emerged in the late 1960s. Politically, it was incarnated in the NDP and the left wing of the Liberal Party; in terms of social forces, the new middle class (in the state and para-state sector) and sections of the trade union movement formed the backbone of opposition to "continentalism," as the American connection was then termed. The new nationalism was on the offensive during much of that period, with government policy in the energy sector, the cultural arena, even foreign policy reflective of this current.

Within Canada, however, there were significant regional variations with respect to nationalism. Alberta, under the Conservatives enjoying a period of unprecedented economic prosperity in the late 1970s and early 1980s, was hostile to any measures that would increase the federal government's role in the energy sector or interfere with the major actors (multinational or smaller Canadian) in the oil patch. Not only did Peter Lougheed react very negatively to the National Energy Program (NEP) introduced by the Trudeau government in late 1980; he also took the initiative of getting the western premiers to call for a free trade deal with the United States a few years later, thus helping to put the issue foursquare onto the political agenda, with the Conservatives in power federally. He also became, following his retirement from Alberta politics, a leading spokesman for the corporate-funded lobby group that pushed the trade deal aggressively. And in electoral terms, Alberta was the one province in English Canada which was to give the Conservatives a majority of the popular vote and an overwhelming majority of the seats in the election (25 of 26), a clear indication of approval for the deal. (I might add that the Reform Party, which received over 15 per cent of votes cast in that province, was also a strong supporter of free trade.)

The other major region of resistance to the new Canadian nationalism was yours, namely Quebec. There is something paradoxical about this, for the Trudeau Liberals stayed in office for fifteen years because of massive majorities in your province. And it was during the Trudeau period that a more nationalist turn in policy could be discerned in a number of areas.

But the major counter-force at the provincial level, the Parti Québécois, was anything but sympathetic to this objective. True, in the early 1970s, Jacques Parizeau, then the party's chief economic adviser, had written the preface to the French language version of Kari Levitt's *Silent Surrender*, a book which denounced American domination of the Canadian economy. And for a short moment, it seemed that Québécois and English Canadian nationalists could agree about the common danger posed by an omnipresent United States.

That moment was not to last, as Parizeau and economists like Rodrigue Tremblay and Bernard Landry were to set their sights on closer integration with the United States. That this was also a means of end-playing English Canada made it so much the more attractive. Since sovereignty for Quebec was the objective, and English Canada the perceived enemy, it followed logically, did it not, that the enemy of one's enemy was one's friend. Cardinal Richelieu had acted no differently during the Thirty Year's War, allying France with Lutheran Sweden against the Catholic Hapsburgs. The PQ would make a similar strategic calculation, preferring the United States – the English-speaking capitalist power par excellence – to the hated Anglos of Canada. (And let us be honest, there is an old elective affinity for the United States over English-speaking Canada buried deep within Quebec popular culture.) René Lévesque's attempts to woo the

New York business community in 1977 were a good forerunner of the position the PQ would take on the free trade deal a decade later. Parizeau, by then its leader, was wont to repeat that free trade would hasten the disintegration of Canada and thereby bring independence for Quebec that much closer.

Robert Bourassa's Liberals were less Richelieuean (or is it Machiavellian?) in their calculations. Their support for free trade by the mid-1980s seemed more firmly rooted in a belief in the advantage this would bring what I call Quebec's new Huguenots (that is, its new entrepreneurial class), and Quebec's resource sector, in particular electricity. Bourassa found himself in the kingmaker's position that he had never enjoyed under Trudeau, who had scarcely disguised his contempt for him (rather justified, now that I think about it!). Mulroney, without a provincial Conservative party in Quebec, was dependent on a combination of Liberal and PQ support to retain that province's allegiance. He was prepared to deal on two key fronts – the constitution and free trade – on both of which Bourassa could pretty well write his own ticket. So during the federal election and the months leading up to it, Bourassa made it clear that his sympathies lay with his friend Brian. This support, in conjunction with that of the PQ and the francophone media, helped secure the Conservative victory, and therefore free trade, in the election.

What is no less striking about the politics of free trade is the crucial support generated for this issue by the one group that above any other enjoys dominant political influence in this country, big business. Forgive the bitterness of my tone, but a key lesson of this election, it seems to me, is that when big business sets its heart on something, it will get its way, whatever popular sentiment may be. The real difference between 1911 and 1988 is that big business opposed reciprocity then, and supported free trade massively this time around. So much for the autonomy of the political, the pluralism of institutional power, in our benighted liberal democracy.

The call for free trade was initiated by groups like the Business Council on National Issues, which represents about 150 of the largest corporations (Canadian and foreign-owned) in this country. The proposal was backed by private think-tanks like the C.D. Howe Institute, itself funded by corporate interests, and eventually won the imprimatur of governmental bodies with an ostensibly arm's-length relationship to big business like the Economic Council of Canada or the Royal Commission on the Economic Union and the Development Prospects for Canada (the Macdonald Commission). One need but look at the briefs from big business to the Macdonald Commission, the relevant chapters of its *Report*, and its preliminary statement extolling the merits of free trade to see the degree to which big business ideology prevailed.

What has changed compared to fifty years ago, we are led to believe, are the trading parameters of the world economy. Canada can no longer get by as a two-bit player, trading with whomever we can find. The world is being carved into trading blocs, and, with our relatively small population and economic base, we have no choice but to link up with a larger economic power. That power can be none other than the United States, a country to which we already direct 70 per cent of our trade, and with which other ties are so close. Our refusal to enter into such an arrangement, we were warned, would see the thunderbolts of protectionism and countervailing duties unleashed on our heads. Ours would become a beggar nation, much weakened and impoverished, incapable of sustaining the levels of economic wealth and corresponding social services to which we had grown accustomed.

A fairly convincing set of arguments, one might think, if we ignore the fact that the Canadian economy had been performing well without a free trade deal throughout the 1980s and showed fair promise of continuing to do so into the 1990s. But there was a further premise to the pro–free trade argument, namely that what is good for big business is good for the country. I happen to agree that Canadian big business stands to gain enormously from the further integration of our two economies, from the newer investment opportunities now opening up south of the border, from the removal or reduction in state regulation and control (generally greater in Canada than in the United States). And our trade union movement, which will find itself up against American "right to work" legislation, give-back wage settlements, and rates of unionization less than half of ours (16 per cent of the American labour force is unionized compared to 37 per cent of the Canadian) cannot but be weakened. If I were Robert Campeau (before his fall!) or David Culver or Conrad Black I would also strongly favour the Canada–US Trade Agreement.

But, as I explained in a previous letter, I remain imbued with a Rousseauean suspicion of the corporate rich. I do not share the envy of ostentatious living which is the stuff of lifestyle magazine littering our doorsteps, nor have I ever assumed that the invisible hand of the market-place, left to itself, would breed anything but forms of inequality as iniquitous as others that had come before. I have never taken the homilies derived from Adam Smith as gospel truth and am no more prepared to believe them today, in societies where it is workers in declining sectors like coal or steel, the homeless of the inner cities, or members of visible minorities who pay the price of the Reagan or Thatcher revolutions. And when one thinks of the international implications of the neo-conservative credo – monetarist policies foisted on the third world by the International Monetary Fund (IMF) and World Bank, food subsidies or wages cut, investment directed to the "haves" in the market sector, environmental degradation – one sees to what a hell the preachings of a Milton Friedman or James Buchanan would reduce the world.

Cher ami, it is because I am *not* a neo-conservative, *not* a believer in market forces *über alles*, *not* convinced that the realm of the political and the realm of the corporate ought to coincide, that I was opposed to the depths of my soul to Canada–us Trade Agreement. For the options this deal closes off – the privileging of values other than individual profit as the be-all and end-all of human existence – are too important to me (and I once thought to you) to be worth so egregious a price.

In truth, the deal was much less about trade than about the model of society we wish for ourselves in the 1990s and beyond. Canadian identity in the postwar era has become more caught up with communitarian values of the liberal-left. Medicare, the Canada Pension Plan, regional equalization programs were some of its symbols, along with the cbc, the Canada Council, or Petro-Canada. Supporters of all these have been disproportionately drawn from the centre and left of the political spectrum and therefore from social forces other than big business.

One need but look at who the key opponents of the trade deal were – trade unions, women's groups, cultural organizations, environmental groups, farmers'organizations, progressive church circles – to see the outline of an alternative set of interests to corporate capital. Many of these interests had spoken out against neo-conservative measures at both the national and provincial level (see the Canadian bishops' statement, "Ethical Reflections on the Economic Crisis" of 1983), arguing for economic approaches that would favour the cooperative and not-for-profit sectors and keep sight of the principles of redistributive justice. For most of these groups, Canadian nationalism was not an end in itself, but the means to the realization (or preservation) of a less dog-eat-dog society in Canada.

The real tragedy of the trade deal, therefore, does not lie in the abstract weakening of Canadian sovereignty. I happen to believe that sovereignty of the Hobbesian variety, in any case, is of diminishing importance in the late twentieth century, and that more and more we must think internationally. But, just as I preferred the internationalism of the student movements to that of the multinational corporation back in the 1960s, so I think it is important to advance progressive social models rather than the neo-conservative one embedded in the Canada–us Trade Agreement. Because I adhere to a more communitarian set of ideals, I reject the homogenizing effects on energy, investment, or labour markets flowing from a comprehensive agreement with as ruggedly capitalistic a power as the United States. (I would, however, have had less of a problem accepting trade liberalization flowing from a more genuinely international set of arrangements like the GATT.) In the absence of a world polity, national boundaries will continue to provide the basis for communitarian endeavours, and for promoting progressive over reactionary values internationally. To that degree, rejection of the deal would have symbolized our choosing a more progressive direction.

The election results suggest that in eight of the provinces majority support ran against the trade deal. True, it is an error to assume that every Liberal or NDP vote was a vote against free trade (a minority within each party favoured the agreement), but, in aggregate, with a combined Liberal-NDP vote of between 55–60 per cent in every province but Alberta, it is reasonable to assume that English Canada en bloc – the Maritimes, Ontario, the West save for Alberta – voted against. It is difficult to attribute motives to this vote. Nationalism clearly played an important role – one thinks of the Turner campaign in particular. But so, in my opinion, did the desire for a less purely market-driven society (witness the risk to medicare and social programs underscored by the Liberals and NDP). What I do know is that the Conservative victory has left deep wounds, and a sense of beleaguered identity through those many parts of English Canada where BMWS and Mercedes do not line the driveways.

We have taken a giant symbolic step closer to the American model. We have reversed twenty years of growing independence – economic, cultural, political – adopting a continental orientation with a vengeance. We have moved from a somewhat more interventionist view of government, from policies modestly favourable to social expenditure and trade union rights, to much more hard-nosed ones. The move to the right which had begun with Mulroney's first term is now likely to be accentuated in ways which will be much more difficult to reverse.

This brings me back to the vote in Quebec, which gave Mulroney his parliamentary majority. The resentment which so many anti–free trade voters in English Canada felt about your vote stems from three things. First, it stems from recognition that yours was the decisive contribution (far more than Alberta's), that with a more even distribution of votes and seats among the three political parties in Quebec, the Conservatives would have been held to a minority or razor-thin majority, insufficient to foist the trade deal on the country. Second, your bloc voting in favour of the winning party, an old Quebec tradition, in fact leads to undue Quebec influence over federal governments, eroding to that degree the influence that other regions, less homogeneous in their voting patterns, can have over what is meant to be their government as well. Third, you voted in this election with supreme indifference to the issues of both Canadian identity and appropriate models of society so clearly posed in the rest of Canada. What mattered to your political elites (and their big business backers) were the gains (real or hypothetical) that Quebec stood to make from the deal. You were ostensibly insulated by language and culture from American influence (I think you greatly underestimate the dangers you face), and would in any case take action to protect *your* national identity were it threatened, witness your government's action following the Supreme Court judgment. But towards *our* national identity (or the question of moderately egalitarian versus neo-conservative choices) your attitude bespoke a sacred egoism bordering on contempt.

I am, no doubt, being unfair, *cher ami*, in lumping together all Québécois, when some 47 per cent of you voted for parties other than the Conservatives. And I know for a fact that many trade unionists, farmers, intellectuals with a critical spirit, ordinary citizens, francophone and anglophone, did not support the trade deal. Clearly, my feelings towards you have in no way been altered because of the election. But I do feel bitterness towards the Claude Charrons and Jacques Parizeaus of this world, towards a whole stratum of self-proclaimed Québécois nationalists whose cynicism with regard to our interests can only breed passionate hostility in reply. I feel bitterness towards Robert Bourassa and his government, insistent on securing a distinct society clause for Quebec whatever the implications for federal-provincial arrangements in the rest of Canada, yet oblivious to the fact that our non-Americanness is what makes English Canada a distinct society. I feel bitterness towards those who wish to have it both ways – always maximizing rights and powers for themselves, disdaining the rights and interests of the "other."

This federal campaign saw a level of political discussion and interest at the grass-roots level without parallel in recent Canadian history. This was no ordinary election, but implicitly a referendum on Canada's future. Free trade became the touchstone of powerful sentiments about Canadian identity, and brought to the fore in English Canada a sense of nationalism that usually lingers far below the surface. It affected Prairie farmers and BC loggers, Maritime lobster fishermen and Ontario autoworkers, Toronto literati, as well as PEI artists and Vancouver cultural activists, and environmentalists and feminists wherever they lived. Such feelings, once aroused, cannot simply be put to rest. Nor will English Canadian nationalists, 1988 vintage, stand idly by and watch the possible demise of our country's core values in the name of the big business agenda. Issues of free trade will dog Canadian politics for years to come, and polarize opinion over and over again, with each plant shutdown, each threatened retreat on social programs or government subsidies, each menace to our cultural fabric.

And like it or not (I do not much like it, but it is a palpable fact), there is a new hostility in the attitude of many English Canadian nationalists towards Quebec. There is a feeling that you have refused to understand English Canada, have allowed the greed of your political and entrepreneurial elites to overcome your better judgment, have precipitated a wrenching readjustment on this country that it may not be able to survive. Already this resentment has claimed an almost certain victim – the Meech Lake Accord. And there may be others. The free trade deal has plunged us into a crisis potentially as acute as the one of which the Preliminary Report of the Royal Commission on Bilingualism and Biculturalism spoke back in 1965.

VIII

Constitutional questions? Already, I can hear the yawn at the other end, and I must admit it is with some trepidation that I raise these myself. God knows, we have had enough of constitutional discussion over the last twenty-five years – amending formulae, special status, division of powers, patriation of the constitution, charter of rights, judicial review versus legislative override. And in the long decades before that, the role of the Judicial Committee of the Privy Council in interpreting the BNA Act ("Peace, order and good government" of section 91 versus "Property and civil rights" of section 92) kept another generation of jurists and scholars busily employed.

There are more interesting questions under the sun, not least, if we want to stick to political ones, regarding ways in which we might make our societies more genuinely democratic than they are. Still, this is Canada and one cannot, in an exchange of letters of this sort, escape the problems that federalism and constitutional arrangements pose for us both. So let me turn to Meech Lake – to what preceded it, to what I think it was all about, and to the reasons that have led to its demise. (I am assuming that it will never come into effect in its original form!)

Some years ago, I wrote an essay called *Parliament vs. People* in which I vented my spleen at the way in which Trudeau had engineered the patriation of the Canadian Constitution and the introduction of the Charter of Rights and Freedoms. My underlying premise was that we have never engaged in democratic constitution-making in this country, and that the 1981 package, worked out, for the most part, by federal and provincial politicians behind closed doors, was a direct heir to the BNA Act, in turn devised by colonial politicians at a series of meetings with no direct reference back to the people. I further accused Trudeau in that essay of constitutional bonapartism for having imposed his own agenda of constitutional reform in the aftermath of the Quebec referendum, with scant acknowledgment of the widespread sentiment within Quebec (even among those who had voted "No") for some tacit recognition of Quebec's specificity within Canada. A few words referring to the "peoples of Canada" or to "the bi-national character of Canada" might well have satisfied this desire and made it difficult for a Quebec government, Péquiste or Liberal, to refuse its assent to the Charter.

Such an acknowledgment, however, would have gone against Trudeau's steadfast opposition to Quebec nationalism and to the "two nations" doctrine throughout his political career. It also would have gone against the grain of his highly ideological liberalism, according to which rights can only be individual, not collective. Thus the Charter is studiously oblivious to social rights (to health, education, or employment), to trade union rights, and to national rights, and the jurisprudence derived from the Charter, for example Supreme Court judgments, is generally similarly biased.

I cannot help feeling that Trudeau, through his actions in 1981–82, is the real author of Meech Lake. I write this perfectly conscious that no one has been as acerbic (and eloquent) in his denunciation of that accord and that many of his criticisms are ones that I agree with. Still, we would not have been into another round of constitutional discussions in 1986–87, if Quebec's assent to the constitutional package of 1981–82 had been secured through appropriate provisions at the time. And there would have always been the possibility, if any of the provinces, including Quebec, had balked, of submitting the entire package for direct approval by the people through referendum – something which would have given it greater legitimacy than it now has.

To be fair to Trudeau, I must reluctantly admit that his constitutional undertaking in 1980–81 was a model of democratic propriety compared with what followed. There was, at least, a joint parliamentary committee that heard hundreds of briefs and introduced some substantive amendments to sections of the Charter. There was, in the final stages, significant input from below, from women's and native organizations in particular, that secured further notable changes. And Trudeau himself (along with Lévesque) in November 1981 was prepared to entertain the idea of holding a referendum before the constitutional package could become law.

The Meech Lake Accord was meant to solve one problem; in fact, it created many others. The brain-child of Gil Rémillard, Robert Bourassa's minister of justice, a man who had criticized the absence of democratic procedures in the 1981–82 constitutional proceedings, and, on the federal side, of officials like Norman Spector who had been Premier Bill Bennett's henchman during the 1983 neo-conservative onslaught in British Columbia, Meech Lake formalized Quebec's status as a "distinct society." This was the key provision meant to rectify the omission of national rights in the Charter and bring Quebec "back into the Constitution." And in the short term it seemed to do the trick. It became the rallying point around which opinion-makers in Quebec and in English Canada – provincial premiers, the leaders of the federal Liberals and NDP – could be brought on board. To speak out against the agreement, in any particular, was to risk being tarred as an enemy of national reconciliation and of Quebec. To proffer possible amendments was to fall into the same trap.

Meech Lake, needless to say, involved a good deal more than the distinct society clause. As the price for winning the consent of the other provincial premiers, for the most part in-

terested in enhancing their own positions, Mulroney was prepared to bargain away a good deal of federal power. For
example, *all* provincial governments would, in future, be able
to opt out of new federal-provincial social programs and secure
appropriate compensation. Future Senate appointments would
be made from lists drawn up by provincial premiers, as would
the appointment of Supreme Court justices. There would be
annual federal-provincial conferences on constitutional matters,
and unanimity rather than the support of seven of the ten provinces would be required for major institutional changes, such
as the admission of new provinces or further Senate reform. In
short, in the name of reconciling Quebec to the Constitution,
there would be a significant weakening of the federal government and a more rigid formula for future constitutional change.

Despite *pro forma* hearings by the parliament of Canada
and various provincial legislatures, there was clearly no room
for changes to this accord. Nor was there any certainty just what
the relationship would be between the distinct society clause
and minority language rights, or indeed any of the other rights,
laid down in the Charter. We were all asked to accept the prom-
ises of Mulroney and the others that all would be for the best
in the best of constitutional worlds. Nor were we to complain
about the highjacking of this and any future constitutional
changes by eleven politicians without any explicit mandate from
the people in whose name they ostensibly acted.

The incredible thing, in retrospect, is how many in English
Canada fell for this arrangement. I confess I was one of them –
sufficiently sensitive to Trudeau's snubbing of Quebec in 1981
to be prepared to swallow the rest in 1987. This, despite the
fact that I found the absence of recourse to a referendum for
direct popular approval of constitutional changes reprehensible,
that I do not want to see the powers of a Bill Vander Zalm (or
any other premier of British Columbia) enhanced by one iota,
that I would much prefer an elected Senate with perhaps a
suspensive veto over Commons legislation to any form of ap-

pointed Senate, and that diluting federally funded social programs or federal spending powers could strengthen neoconservative impulses in the regions.

We are sometimes blinded to the full implications of our positions. And though I heard and read Trudeau's denunciations of Meech Lake, of how it would emasculate the federal government, I was sufficiently outraged by his high-handed action five years before to dismiss these as the jeremiads of a biased observer. All this until 21 November.

Then it hit me with the force of a ton of bricks. Here you were in Quebec – Robert Bourassa in the lead – ensuring that free trade would be rammed down our collective throats by a government with only two-fifths of the popular vote outside Quebec. Here was our identity, forged painstakingly out of resisting the blandishments and encroachments of the United States for over 120 years, up for grabs. Here was the ability of the Canadian government to limit American incursions into our resource sector, our service sector, even our social programs, severely curtailed. And here you were, asking us to further prune the powers of the federal government through Meech Lake in order to recognize *your* distinct identity. Moreover, we were to congratulate ourselves for the wonderful deal we were getting in the process.

On the night of 21 November, it became clear to me (and to many others) that we had been living in a fool's paradise. You (I mean the majority of Québécois) could not give a damn for our concerns, for our nationality; all that mattered to you was your own. For almost thirty years we had been hearing about how badly Quebec had been treated by English Canada, how your survival within North America was on the line, why you needed special powers and perhaps sovereignty itself to maintain your identity. And when *for once* our identity was in jeopardy, when it was our turn to ask your help in allowing *both* our societies to continue with a modicum of independence vis-à-vis the United States, your answer was a resounding "No."

Meech Lake began to unravel almost at once. It no longer made sense for us to violate some of our most cherished principles to accommodate a partner so churlish in return. Why pay the slightest attention to Gil Rémillard's threats ("No other constitutional negotiations if Meech Lake fails") or Bourassa's insipid observations ("The opposition to Meech Lake is a temporary fit of pique on the part of the opponents of free trade") when we had only our own interests to consider. We had learned from you overnight that selfishness alone mattered, that any concessions we made would be unilateral unless and until you began to take our own interests half as seriously as we had been taking yours. If the gloves were off on your side, they sure as hell would come off on ours.

Three days after the election, the leader of the NDP in Manitoba announced that his party would not support Meech Lake. Gary Doer, along with Sharon Carstairs, the Liberal Leader in Manitoba, spoke for millions of English Canadians who were convinced that the country could not afford both free trade and Meech Lake. They spoke for millions who did not want any further devolution of federal powers to the provinces. And they spoke for millions who felt that the absence of meaningful popular input into the Meech proceedings and the top-down style of constitution-making that it incarnated stank.

The rest is now history. The Conservative premier of Manitoba, responding to Bourassa's override of the Supreme Court judgment, himself announced the withdrawal of the Meech resolution from his legislature. And it suddenly became clear that English-language minority rights in Quebec, like French Canadian minority rights in the rest of Canada, are of larger national concern, and cannot be superseded in the name of a "distinct society," not without delivering a mortal blow to the notion of bilingualism and biculturalism which has underlain Canadian federalism for the last twenty years.

And we are back to square one. Will we become a Swiss-style federation, with Bill 101 and other legislation progressively whittling away the use of English in Quebec, until the province becomes de facto unilingual? In turn, will English Canada become increasingly sceptical about French minority rights and about the use of Canada's other official language within its borders? This scenario is a real possibility, as is the sort of nastiness Belgium has come to know in linguistic matters. Alternatively, do we want to maintain a reasonable degree of toleration for our two linguistic minorities – or should we call them hostages – and for each other's distinct character and interests?

I keep harping back to this point. The real lesson from the linking of free trade and Meech Lake is that the actions of the one society have consequences for the other – whether each is fully conscious of it or not. You cannot wilfully ignore our sentiments on free trade and expect us to blithely allow you to get your way on constitutional reform. We cannot impose our vision of federalism or Canadian nationalism on you, if your interpretation of your interests pulls you in the opposite direction. If we are to live together, we will have to recognize the principle of reciprocity in our relationship. It cannot be all take, take, take on the one side and give, give, give on the other.

The 21 November election represents a crossroad in English Canadian attitudes towards Quebec. We are no longer prepared to offer you unlimited concessions, while overlooking our own fundamental interests. We have no reason to apologize for our commitment to a reasonably strong central state – the embodiment of English Canadian identity – nor will we bargain it away to please Mulroney, Bourassa, or anyone else. We are prepared to take bilingualism and biculturalism seriously, but we expect you to do the same. This does not mean you cannot take measures to promote or protect the French language in Quebec. But it does mean we cannot have one set of principles for minority rights for English Canada and a wholly different one for Quebec. If you ignore our legitimate concerns in this regard, do not expect us to cater to yours.

Already, I hear veiled threats in the background of sovereignty-association or out-and-out independence. These do not frighten me. There are many, especially in western Canada, who would probably find sovereignty-association attractive at this point. It would remove some of the poison from our blood-stream, they would argue. As for Quebec independence, all this would mean is that each of our two solitudes would Americanize at its own pace, you with what remains of your language to shroud your identity, we with our vestigial attachment to less individualistic values than the United States.

Yet, *cher ami*, it is too easy to erase 120 years of life together, as though only mutual hatred could mark our paths. Nor am I writing you these letters to give petulance free reign. I am fully conscious of the hard realities that face us both in the brave new world of free trade *and* constitutional discord about to unfold. If we are to survive as viable communities, it will only be if each of us is prepared to balance self-interest with due respect for the legitimate interests of the other. You have been less good at doing this in recent years than we have. A line from Rilke comes to mind: "You must change your life."

IX

What precisely might it mean – to change collective attitudes at this late date? Acknowledging that one can be no less attached to one's community of language and culture, one's nation, while treating the other community of language and culture with which one must cohabit seriously? Accepting that there are values which cut across linguistic boundaries, that may unite us in common objectives and interests as members of the human race, of an increasingly polluted planet, and of a world crying out for a more just distribution of goods and resources between north and south? Adhering to a universal framework of rights, without a notwithstanding clause I might add?

Cher ami, I do not share the dream of Trudeau and his generation of remaking Canada into a bilingual and bicultural society from coast to coast. (I think it did lie in the back of their minds as a model to be pursued.) Nor do I, for one moment, assume that the vast majority of members of one linguistic community can ever acquire the kind of intimate knowledge of another language and culture that allows them to truly feel at home in it. Rare individuals may be able to make the passage, or like the *philosophes* of the eighteenth century live in a world of discourse above the hurly-burly of national divisions. To expect the ordinary anglophone from Calgary or francophone from Chicoutimi to understand just what it means to "live" in Quebec or Alberta, to absorb the shared patterns and traditions that go into the making of *mentalités*, is to engage in sociological fantasy. It is, as Rousseau argued in another context, to posit a society of angels, not men and women.

What is less utopian, however, is to ask for a little curiosity about a neighbouring society, especially when one shares with that society a political structure, economic framework, and social system. I do not mean by this the superficial familiarity that comes from spending a week-end in Toronto or Montreal, attending a business or professional or trade union convention every now and then, or sending teenagers from one of our linguistic groups to spend a couple of weeks living with the other. All this may be gratifying for those involved, but rarely leaves much that endures.

I am thinking about the need for sustained interest, one that would find expression in the textbooks we use in our elementary and secondary schools, in the teaching and research going on in our universities, in our newspapers and magazines, radio and television programming, in both high brow and popular culture. Such a focus does not mean ceasing to be concerned with what makes each of us unique. But it suggests some opening to the interests of the other, tacit recognition that there are after all two major linguistic and cultural communities in this country.

As an English Canadian academic with a sustained interest in Quebec, I have no doubt been in a privileged position to follow your debates, immerse myself in the writings of your social scientists, pay some attention to shifting currents in your cultural life. And there have been others from English Canada – journalists, historians, educators, literary critics – who have paid you the supreme compliment of taking you as seriously as you take yourselves. Some of this has also penetrated, slowly and unevenly I am prepared to admit, into the textbook treatments in English Canada of phenomena like the Quiet Revolution or the 1980 referendum, the conscription crises of the two world wars, the Manitoba school question, or the hanging of Riel. The interpretation placed on these events has not always been the same as yours, but the events have not been ignored, nor has your viewpoint.

If I do have a bone to pick with you, it is that I fail to find a matching interest for English Canada within your intellectual community. Where are your experts on English Canadian political life, on Canadian, as opposed to Quebec, history, on our literary or cultural evolution? How much space is given to Canadian, as opposed to Quebec, themes in your elementary or secondary school texts? How many of your academics have spent any time at English Canadian universities or paid much attention to our debates? How much coverage is there in *Le Devoir* or *La Presse* of developments in English Canada, except when they directly impinge on you?

It is odd, methinks, that there is so little opening to the rest of Canada. I know your population is only about a third of ours, that you have had other preoccupations – legitimate preoccupations, I hasten to add – over the last three decades, that language is as much a barrier for many of you as it is for many of us. Yet your university bookstores are stacked with English-language texts in economics and microbiology, your journalists have spent time in Ottawa or New York as well as Paris, your social scientists have travelled the four corners of the globe. Is it really too much to ask that by now at least a handful of you might have begun to pay us the compliment of taking English Canada seriously?

The problem, I am convinced, is that you have become excessively self-centred. And here nationalism can have deleterious, rather than positive, effects. For while nationalism provides the sense of identity and cultural bonding so vital to intellectual creation – the 1960s is there to prove it in Quebec – it can also, when pushed to excess, close off a necessary interaction with members of any other national grouping. Intellectual exchange becomes impossible, alternative explanations or approaches too alien to grasp, terms of discourse solipsistic in the extreme. Why risk challenging sacred cows by engaging in dialogue outside the circle of the elect?

In a way, if you forgive me the parallel, such closed thinking is not unlike what the Roman Catholic Church practised through many long centuries in its attitude towards those of another faith. Whether Moslem, Protestant, East Orthodox, Jewish or, worst of all, freethinker, there was no possible discourse between the community of the faithful and those of heretical views. Contact with another mode of thinking or belief would inevitably shatter the certitudes upon which one's theology had been constructed. The sin of relativism opened the door to eternal perdition.

We fortunately live in a more ecumenical age, in which religious faith is not incompatible with tolerance for those of a different persuasion. A Galileo today would not be condemned for astronomical heterodoxy, nor the works of a Voltaire or Diderot placed on the *Index liborum prohibitorum*. The church itself has become more tolerant, and our societies increasingly secular and pluralistic in their values.

Surely, we do not need political orthodoxies to replace the religious ones of yesterday. We know where Marxism-Leninism brought Soviet society during the period of Stalin or Brezhnev, what Nazism spelled for intellectual life (and all life) in Germany, or what, in a milder way admittedly, McCarthyism meant for the United States in the early 1950s. In similar fashion, a closed national discourse, convinced of the absolute truths that it holds, can prove inimical to the interests of the society it claims to protect.

I do not want to exaggerate. Quebec society today, as we all know, is not monolithic. There is real diversity to your political and social life, and, on issues like abortion, homosexuality, or pornography, possibly a greater degree of individual toleration than in English Canada, with Puritan residues to its culture. But there are tendencies, especially where nationalism is concerned, to a "party line" that imposes a particular view of the "nation" as the one that any self-respecting francophone must accept. It assumes, for example, that there is a zero-sum game between the use of French in Quebec and minority linguistic rights, between "collective" and "individual" rights. To suggest that it might be possible to reconcile the two, to continue to promote French as the dominant language in Quebec without reducing the status of English to that of a pariah tongue, is to offend against the consensus. To listen to the views of English Canadians – inside or outside Quebec – is to listen to the heretic.

You need an end to Manichean-type thinking, to anathemas directed against this or that mode of thought. And here, an opening to English Canada might actually do your intellectual and political life some good. One thing you – or that handful of journalists or academics who paid us some attention – would notice is that even on nationalism, perhaps especially on nationalism, there is a great diversity of opinion. During the free trade debate, for example, a majority of economists in English Canada and a certain number of other academics embraced closer trading ties with the United States as the supreme good. Yet a goodly number of others took precisely the opposite position. There are Canadian intellectuals who identify with regionalism, others more committed to a strong central government. Our artists and writers, though for the most part favouring nationalism, include some who take the opposite stance.

We all have views we hold dear – and what would intellectual life be like if we did not? But there ought to be room for a diversity of views on all important subjects, no taboo topics on which discussion is foreclosed before it can even begin. I am not asking you to abandon long-held views on Quebec nationalism or on how best to advance the cause of the French language in Quebec. But I am asking you to recognize that even on this there can be legitimate differences of opinion, that those who adopt another position have not placed themselves outside the pale of national debate. You went through an excruciating referendum campaign on the future of Quebec in the spring of 1980. Were Solange Chaput-Rolland or Claude Ryan or Pierre Trudeau, for that matter, less authentically Québécois than René Lévesque or Camille Laurin?

What is sauce for the goose is naturally sauce for the gander. Whatever my own strong feelings against the free trade deal, I cannot, in good conscience, claim that those who supported it were somehow less genuinely Canadian, mere agents for a foreign land. Conspiracy theories of this sort may be convenient, but they avoid the bedrock reality of conflicting interests and ideological positions in a complex society such as ours. I would not want English Canadian nationalism to be intolerant, any more than I think you ought to want Quebec nationalism to be.

One way to avoid that intolerance is to have to take the interests of another community into account. I know for a fact – despite my pique about the way the majority of you voted on 21 November – that my vision of Canadian nationalism has always left room for a strong and resilient French Canadian nationalism alongside. I think that we in English Canada learned some of our nationalism from you in the late 1960s, and that, in a more profound way, we have been marked by Canada's cultural dualism. While one can imagine an English-speaking Canada without Quebec, it would certainly be a Canada with a less open form of nationalism than we have today.

You too have more to gain from our coexistence than you have been willing to let on. I am not just talking about hard dollars and cents – markets, aggregate federal spending, and the like. Nor about foreign policy, where, for example, Canada can make a more significant contribution to *la francophonie* than Quebec by itself (something Mitterrand seems to understand better than did de Gaulle). In the past, your sense of nation was forged in resistance to possible assimilation by ours. The tension between our two nations has, in an odd sort of way (that the Machiavelli of *The Discourses* or the Madison of *The Federalist Papers* might have understood), helped to keep your own identity more strongly alive. Yet if tension is a permanent feature of federalism – especially where two or more nationalities are involved – it also follows that there can be mutual enrichment from the contact. Would medicare have been introduced so quickly into Quebec if it had not first been tried in Saskatchewan? Would secularization have taken hold overnight if there had not been the model of a more secular society cheek by jowl with Quebec? Would there have been the same vogue for educational reform in the 1960s had it not been apparent that Quebec was light-years behind the rest of the country?

In the same spirit, I think you have things to learn from us today. We are not all stereotypical, cold, calculating rationalizers; on the contrary, as the free trade debate showed, many of us are profoundly attached to communitarian values that should attract those of you who hark back (or think forward) to less market-driven values. We have fairly developed artistic and scientific traditions, and a spirit of give and take in our intellectual exchanges that merits more than passing interest on your part. We are not simply another version of Americans, and to that degree, we can help you to resist the homogenizing attraction of the great power we live beside – if you are really serious about preserving your identity.

My point, *cher ami*, is that you need, as a society, to reconsider your position towards us. A defensive reflex and siege mentality towards English Canadians is out of date. The cold indifference, larded with generous gobs of self-interest, that has underlain your position on constitutional questions, or more recently on free trade, will also pay diminishing returns. English Canadians are not without an *amour propre* to match your own.

It will do you a world of good to start taking some interest in the other Canada that *we* live in. You will not be worse Québécois for it, or in any way likely to exchange your identity for ours. But it should make you more open, more sensitive to the fact that federalism is a two-way street and dualism dependent on the coexistence of partners with some consciousness of what makes the other different.

In no way would I ask for more. And it goes without saying that a reasonable openness on our part to your interests will be called for. This, by itself, will not resolve such outstanding matters as your status within the Canadian Constitution or the relationship between "collective" and "individual" rights within your own society. But it might, at least, begin to move us beyond the impasse in which we presently find ourselves.

X

I am coming to the end of this correspondence, and cannot help wondering whether it is likely to have the slightest effect. You are not used to listening to voices from English Canada, however well disposed, and at points in these letters – how can I deny it? – rancour has crept in. You consider yourself to be a person without prejudice, *sans parti pris*, yet here I am suggesting that you have been remarkably closed minded on a series of issues – bilingualism and biculturalism, the constitution, free trade – where English Canadians have interests of their own to advance. "Some friend," you have probably been muttering under your breath. "Scratch an English Canadian, even of the left, and you will find an unreconstructed federalist vision of Canada. The Trudeau-Chrétien line all over again, with a thick layer of *angst* or outrage to help him cover his tracks."

Cher ami, you will hold whatever opinion you wish to hold of me. My protests will be to no avail. And if your preferred response is to pigeon-hole what I have to say, to dismiss it with a sweep of the hand or shrug, what more should I have expected? A contrite admission on your part that perhaps you have interpreted us wrongly, taken us too much for granted, pressed legitimate interests beyond the limit? There will be no 4 August 1789 of Canadian federalism, no miraculous renunciation of privileges or reconciliation of provinces, no easy agreement as to who is the aggrieved party and who the offender in our binational tandem. The most these letters may have convinced you of is that there is another side.

There are a number of other issues I would like to raise before bidding you a fond farewell. They have to do less with the nature of our two nationalisms or with our recent differences than with matters on which we both need to think long and hard if we are to avoid an atrophied political life. Make no bones about it – to allow the corporate sector, anglophone *and* francophone, to run away with the political agenda, to assume, for one moment, that we can safely cede all power to our elected governments and get back to pursuing purely private interests, is to abdicate our responsibilities as democratic citizens.

Democracy, if we go back to the Greeks for a moment, was intimately caught up with the notion of equality. There was the equality of citizenship rights, or, if one prefers, equality before the law. There was the equal right of citizens to partake in the deliberations of the sovereign assembly, a right that went well beyond the ritual one we partake in every three or four years of casting votes during elections. And there was also, for some at least, a notion of equal division of the land, or if you wish, equality of condition, something which provokes the deepest political and philosophical cleavage between left and right down to today.

All these dimensions of democracy have potential relevance for our society. Yet we have a relatively thin notion of what citizenship is all about, far less demanding than was the liberty of the ancients. In Canada, we are heirs to a rigidly Burkean notion of sovereignty that would cede to our elected parliamentarians and ministers plenipotentiary power. We have rarely had direct popular input into decision-making, be it with respect to the constitution (1867, 1982, 1987) – or to other important issues of the day.

There have been a few exceptions to this which, here and there, have allowed a slightly more Rousseauean notion of sovereignty to find expression. One important strand of this was Prairie populism which, in the first decades of this century, pushed strongly for notions like legislative recall and delegate democracy, both of which would have made legislatures and governments more responsive to the direct will of the electorate. Another strand has been referenda – both the plebiscite on conscription held in 1942 and, more tellingly still, the sovereignty-association referendum you held in Quebec in 1980 to determine your constitutional option for the future. In Quebec, at least, there seemed to be close to universal acceptance of the proposition that on a matter of such importance to the whole population only a direct expression of the popular will, outside the framework of legislative elections, could really be determining.

I devoutly wish we had gone the same route with respect to free trade, not because the outcome would necessarily have been different from the one 21 November gave us. Public opinion on the issue was close to evenly divided and might well have gone either way. But in a referendum, the electorate would have been obliged to give its unstinted attention to the Canada–US Trade Agreement, without simultaneously having to make up its mind as to which political party was to govern for the next four years. A referendum would have provided the issue with the solemnity it deserved, underlining the fact that Canadians were faced with a historic choice in their relationship with the United States, one which they themselves should decide directly (as the Norwegians, Danes, and British were to decide with respect to membership in the European Community). The result of a referendum, moreover, is unambiguous, with 50 per cent plus 1 of the vote for one side or the other. There could then be no disputing the legitimacy of the result in the way that opponents of the deal, with some validity, can question the Mulroney government's mandate.

What ought we to do if we are indeed to introduce more direct democracy into this country? Ought we to be holding referenda on all contentious matters, and especially constitutional changes? Ought we to be empowering citizen groups or public interest movements to bring contentious issues before the public and, where sufficient interest is expressed (for example through the appropriate number of signatures on petitions), to trigger a referendum mechanism? Ought we to be promoting more extensive forms of democracy within publicly funded organizations (social agencies, health services, institutions of higher learning, crown corporations), within the corporate sector (perhaps through worker-elected directors on governing boards), and at the grass-roots or local level throughout society?

Clearly there is subject matter here for wide-ranging debate. It seems to me that it is something you in Quebec, no less than we in English Canada, have reason to address, that it undercuts the familiar bombast which politicians use, once elected, to arrogate onto themselves powers which we, the people, do not necessarily wish to cede. Is the Westminster model we have inherited from Great Britain, with its tendency to give a winning party (usually with only a plurality of the votes) a crushing majority in terms of seats, a truly democratic system? Should even a government that garners a majority of the popular vote, as occasionally happens, be able to interpret this as a *carte blanche* to do anything it wishes during its term of office? Here we have important things to learn from the Greeks, from Rousseau, from Jefferson, from the Paris Commune of 1871, from the experience of Switzerland, Australia, or a number of American states.

There is a related question that arises with respect to democracy, and that is the place of money in our political life, or should I not really say our society. The problem here is not the straightforward one of controlling election expenditures so that a party with strong corporate backing, for example, cannot outspend its opponents by a factor of three or four to one. We have made some progress over the past few decades in limiting such expenditures at the federal level and in several of the provinces. There is still room for significant abuse, mind you, when one thinks of the gross overspending on advertising by the pro–free trade forces in the recent election as compared to the much smaller sums available for advertising by opponents of the deal.

My concerns regarding the corrupting influence of wealth, however, run a good deal deeper. I am convinced that we will continue to operate within a system where the dice are unfairly loaded *all the time*, as long as we allow the ratios of inequality in wealth that exist at present (10 to 1 or 20 to 1 between income earners in the top and bottom income brackets) to continue. I am not arguing for some kind of *absolute* equality of condition, which would entail, among other things, so repressive a political authority as to be incompatible with any form of liberal democracy. Nor would I belittle, on straight economic grounds, the importance of incentives, and, therefore, of a degree of inequality in our societies. This is, in fact, the lesson that some of the comrades to the east seem to be learning, as they try to move away from an excessively centralized and planned model of the economy.

But, even as Marxist-Leninist regimes begin to liberalize and, we hope, democratize, we in the west must be careful not to chuck out the principle of equality as inherent to the democratic project. There has been, as welfare theorists like T.H. Marshall argued, a movement from purely legal notions of citizenship in western societies of the eighteenth century, to political citizenship with the extension of the franchise, to more social notions in the twentieth century, as exemplified by the welfare state. We are at a crossroad, where forces of the right, opposed to equality, would attempt to reverse that trend, downgrading the social component of citizenship as much as possible.

I have already told you that my strongest reservations about the trade deal stem from the fact that it threatens to align Canadian society more directly on American. Whatever else the United States has been in the late twentieth century, it has not been the home of a more social notion of citizenship, of a welfare society or state. Nor has equality of condition found much support from the mainstream of the American political establishment, Republican or Democratic. I do not want to overestimate the degree of support that might exist for this within Canada – even our Liberals tend to make "equality of opportunity" the limit of their credo. Yet they have been pressured (or cajoled), usually by the CCF or NDP, into accepting slightly more redistributive elements into certain programs. And we do, as a society, both in English Canada and Quebec, have a less purely individualistic set of values than do the Americans.

The task, now that free trade is upon us, is to prevent the further erosion of this communitarian strain. Allowing market forces to take their toll will decimate the unionized sectors of the work force and put enormous pressure on governments to trim excessive expenditure (excessive by American standards, it goes without saying). Big business, both yours and ours, will be leading the attack. Changes to the unemployment insurance system introduced in April 1989 and cuts in social spending in the Wilson budget of the same month are proof enough of this.

So you can no more afford to rest on your laurels, assuming that the social gains of the Quiet Revolution are secure, than can we on ours. Each generation is forced to refight the battle for social justice, on terms and conditions not always of its own choosing. Our antagonist in this round is neo-conservatism, a philosophy that favours individual interests and widening social inequality as the motor of economic and social change.

We are, as I acknowledged in an earlier letter, no longer confronting purely domestic forces. There are larger tendencies in the world economy for capitalist restructuring and consolidation and for more market-driven public policies. We have seen this at work in the United States and United Kingdom and, in a less crusading manner, in continental Europe and in Japan. International agencies like the IMF, the World Bank and the Organization for Economic Co-operation and Development have helped spread the gospel far and wide, and we in Canada have not escaped it.

Still, I have never been defeatist or assumed that the proper response to the offensive of the marketeers was to retreat into one's tent. *Au contraire*, it is precisely when the current seems to be going in the opposite direction that it is necessary to prepare a counter-offensive, first intellectually, then in the political and economic arenas.

There are wide chinks in the armour of the new right that need to be exploited. The most basic, which we too easily overlook, is that their view of human nature is profoundly flawed in abstracting out the social dimension of our existence and placing supreme emphasis on our individual attributes. That we are born into societies, moulded by them, nurtured within family units, linked to our fellow citizens by political bonds, which may involve our willingness to lay down our lives, entirely escapes the Christopher Columbuses of monetarism and public choice.

Their second major error is to engage in a form of economic reductionism which, in an odd sort of way, mimes the economic determinism long practised by a certain Marxist orthodoxy. The laws of the economic market-place are read into our political arrangements. Our votes are much like the cash or credit cards we carry in our wallets, to be expended on political goods that catch our fancy. The closer a political party (or government) comes to satisfying our rational economic need for public goods, the more successful it will be. Remarkably little scope is given in such a theory for non-economic forms of behaviour, for example, those inspired by political ideology, ethnicity, religion, or the *libido dominandi* of rulers. It provides a poor explanation of the politics of any of the major twentieth-century states, with the possible exception of the United States, and as a predictive theory it is extraordinarily simplistic.

Their third error is to underestimate the efficacy of state action. Because social spending ran up against the barrier of declining economic growth in the 1970s and therefore fiscal crisis, it followed that social expenditures were in and of themselves a permanent drag on economic development that needed to be cut. No matter if the consequences were to increase anomy throughout the lower levels of society, or to cut into basic services such as health and education, whose short- and long-term effects for economic well-being are inestimable. Because regulation got in the way of profit-making, it followed that one should loosen up on environmental standards, airline safety, etc. Because private was by definition better than public, one should sell off all state enterprises, even if the social objectives public corporations can serve (service to peripheral communities, good wages and working conditions for their employees, reasonable fare structures, service in two official languages) may simultaneously go out the window.

I do not want to defend every state activity as a good in itself; I do think that we must find ways to make the public sector more responsive to community input and control from below. Indeed, this is precisely what the left in Europe and here in North America has been increasingly advocating, as it looks to less-statist alternatives to traditional social democratic nostrums for the economy. But to assume that a simple-minded commitment to "getting the state off our backs" will resolve the social, economic, and environmental ills that afflict our society or the world at large is absurd.

Cher ami, I could go on, but I wonder whether I have to persuade you that these are questions that transcend our familiar linguistic or cultural quarrels. The constellation of social forces that came together in English Canada in opposition to free trade – trade unions, women's groups, environmentalists, the cultural community, farmers' organizations – is no different from the popular movements in Quebec that oppose the unsullied reign of your entrepreneurial class. We can only gain from fruitful contact with each other, and from making common cause where larger national and international questions are concerned.

I do not want to end on an unrealistic note. I am fully aware of what has stood in the way of cooperation between the left (or liberal-left) in English Canada and that of Quebec, namely the national question. This cannot simply be wished away, witness our rather different responses to the issues of free trade and Bill 178. And try as we may to be civil, or even cordial, to one another, there will remain intractable differences between the ways in which you look on Canada (and Quebec's place within it) and the way we in English Canada see the country.

Yet can we really afford the luxury of speaking past rather than to each other? There would be only one beneficiary – big business – and many losers. There would be only one kind of economic agenda – the one we have seen unfolding in the United States and Britain. There would be one party in power at the national level – anchored to the right of the political spectrum. There would be one prevailing vision of society – rooted in starkly atomistic values. *Cher ami*, when we meet again, will this be all we see as we scan the horizon? Or will you in Quebec have joined your efforts to ours in beginning to formulate more humane and compelling alternatives for the coming decade?

Betrayal and Indignation on the Canadian Trail: A Reply from Québec

Daniel Latouche

This much is clear. You feel betrayed

You feel betrayed mostly because of Meech Lake and its distinct society clause, but also because of the 1988 free trade election where apparently we voted on the wrong side and of Bill 178 which restricts the use of English in outdoor advertising. The Québécois have let you down! You warn us therefore, in no uncertain terms, that things will never be the same between us, that is between Canada and Québec. Something has changed, you write, "something which will leave an indelible mark on this country for a generation." We have made life impossible for those of you who, as you put it, "in the recent past, were most sympathetic to Québec and its national aspirations. " (I hope you do not mind if I put back the *accent aigue* on Québec, *une question d'habitude*.) Who do we think we are? you ask.

You feel betrayed and indignant at our lack of understanding and interest in English Canada. Québec, Québec, Québec all the time and never satisfied.

Will it ever end? English Canada is striving for recognition, for some acknowledgment by the Québécois of "the kind of society and people" you really are. And what do we offer in return: *ignorance, mépris, indifférence, paternalisme*. Indignation and a sense of betrayal: in other words you are mad as hell.

What do you expect from us? What does English Canada want? (Does the question ring a bell?) You appear to want us to plead guilty on all counts, recognize our sins, and proceed to mend our collective Québec ways. Quite a program, I might say. If this is indeed what you want, allow me to present some ex post facto explanations and a bit of plea bargaining.

GRATITUDE AS A WAY OF LIFE

You have made serious charges and I will take them seriously, although at times I must admit I find it difficult. "You did not use the back of the spoon" (as we say in Quebec). But your indignation wears a bit thin. Something terrible must have happened to turn you into an admiring and a repentant disciple of Pierre Trudeau. Remember him? He is the man who brought us the War Measures Act, wage and price controls, and the 1982 Constitution. I never thought I would see the day when you confessed to having been blind to his profound wisdom.

Who said that nothing ever changed on the Canadian ideological range? Your conversion leads me to believe that there must be more to it than mere annoyance at a constitutional package which everyone agrees changes absolutely nothing. The free trade election of 1988? It is true that we supported the Conservatives of Brian Mulroney, but you have to admit we had little choice. Have you ever considered the alternative from our perspective? Could we possibly have voted for the party of Jean Chrétien or for the NDP? The Liberals are still a bad joke in Québec, and we knew perfectly well that with them in power we would end up with another free trade deal, one that used the pretext of renegotiation with the Americans to put Québec in its place. You do not really want to hear me on the subject of the NDP and so I will say no more of it for the moment.

As I have just said, we did look at the free trade election from a Québec perspective. But what other perspective could we have used? That of the Canadian economy and culture? But, we are only guests in this great land of yours. And you never miss a chance to remind us that our lease is up. You are quick to say that our vision is not a Canadian one. Do you mean to

imply that yours is? I do not speak for Canada, and few Québécois would claim to do so. But what makes you so sure of
your 20–20 Canadian vision? I am no great fan of Canadian
federalism – that is an understatement – but who are you to tell
me that my vision of the country is wrong simply because my
glasses are québécois? You reinvent the rules and rearrange the
furniture and expect me to know my way around. I must have
been looking in some other direction the day the directive came
down from the desk of the reconstituted Waffle and proclaimed
that from now on the test of true Canadianness would include
a question on free trade.

And then, there is Bill 178, the most ridiculous piece of
legislation ever passed in Canada. It turns Québec into a linguistic Disneyland, French on the outside and English inside.
And in doing so it tears down the only clause of Bill 101 still
standing. I refuse to believe that you failed to see the consequences of such a law. It takes us back twenty years. Is this what
you want?

Robert Bourassa and his gnomes want to turn Québec into
a bilingual zoo. Do not kid yourself. Their aim is bilingualism of
the worst kind, and they would have pressed it had Québécois,
young and old, separatists and federalists, socialists and feminists, not woken up at the last minute. But when will you English
Canadians get it through your thick collective skull that we want
to live in a French society, inside and outside, at work and at
play, in church and in school. Is this so difficult to understand?
Do you get some kind of secret satisfaction from forcing us to
repeat this simple fact time after time?

You appear to believe that we are worried about one lone
English sign buried deep in Westmount. That you think my knees
begin to shake when I see an English sign is quite insulting. I
do not see red either. Your belief is irrational so how can I even
begin to set you straight. I can only reassure you: one sign, two
signs, a thousand signs do not worry me. This is not the point
and you know it. What would you say if all the signs in downtown

Vancouver, on Granville and Robson, at Eaton's and at every White Spot were suddenly written in both Cantonese and English. What would you say if every third store you walked into you were welcomed in Cantonese. Add to this the fact that half your radio and television stations are in Cantonese and that most of your government ministers cannot explain to you, in your own language, what they are doing with your taxes. Would you not, at the very least, ask yourself: "Where am I?"

My example probably makes you uncomfortable. One never talks of such things in Canada, especially since I cannot claim that some of my best friends are Cantonese. Like you, I know full well what kind of attitudes usually lie behind talk of too many immigrants, too fast. Under no circumstance will I excuse discriminatory attitudes and practices, nor will I allow people to tell me that this is North America and we should forget about this "French thing."

Do not lecture me on humiliation or on the futility of trying to help my cause by putting down the next guy. I know everything there is to know about humiliation and what the next guy really wants. Our vision of what a French society is clearly different. No reconciliation is possible I am afraid. For you a French society is one where French-speaking Canadians can find work in French, buy their groceries in French, and watch television or go to school in French. When you think of a French society you think of a Chinatown-like situation. This is precisely how Americans see it. This is how they see Canada and especially English Canada. Their vision of society is purely individualistic, based on the sharing of material goods and infused with patriotic symbols. But I was wrong when I assumed this vision is still prevalent in English Canada. The free trade debate has shown that for a growing number of English Canadians there is more to a Canadian society and a Canadian culture than the mere symbols of sovereignty. Why do you not see how similar the situation is in Québec?

If there is a reason to be upset about the Supreme Court ruling against Bill 101, it is because of the nonchalant way in which the judges borrowed from the American legal tradition and elevated commercial signs into symbols of free speech and fundamental freedoms. The Québec government should be commended for standing up to a court, supreme or not, which dared a constitutionally elected government to use a legal and legitimate clause of the Constitution, the notwithstanding clause. You may be surprised at this interpretation of Québec's recent use of the notwithstanding clause, but by claiming that the outdoor advertising section of Bill 101 was illegitimate, illegal, tyrannical, and undemocratic, the court has taken upon itself to encourage the non-respect of any follow-up legislation based on the "notwithstanding" clause.

We are talking of the Canadian Constitution, the law of the land. How can it bring shame on those who abide by it? How can we be blamed for making use of one of its articles, fully respecting the spirit and the wording of the document? Or is it that everything Québec touches is automatically tainted?

By what right do these judges tell us, Canadians and Québécois, how they are so unhappy with some of the constitutional rules devised by our elected representatives, that they feel the need to point out, ahead of time, that the only possible use for these rules is to cover up injustice and tyranny. What a comment on Canada, the Canadian Constitution, and the Canadian political order! What kind of country puts in its constitutional books an escape clause that is only a trap to bring shame on its eventual user. What would your reaction have been if the clause had been used by the federal government to circumvent a Supreme Court ruling preventing women from obtaining an abortion or even from making use of contraceptives? Would you have cried "Foul!" with the same intensity?

Your anger is selective.

Your silence is a comment on what you believed to be the immaturity of the Canadian people who have to suffer under this order and who nevertheless insist on re-electing the same representatives. You of all people should have objected to this legal blackmail and affirmation that judges are above the law of the land and the will of the people. Not to mention the fact that they did so to protect commercial interests thus accelerating the judicial integration of Canada within the American legal culture. How can you remain silent when provincial leaders claim that a clause of the Canadian Constitution cannot be used by a Québec premier? What next? Will it become unacceptable for native people to use the court system and the Charter of Rights because they do not recognize the moral authority of the federal government with sufficient zeal?

How could you fail to see the implications of this ruling? Are you in such awe of the justices that you fail to see their primitive grab for power? They are mere mortals after all. In the past, you did not sanctify the Charter of Rights and the Supreme Court. How often did you point to the biased nature of their decisions, especially towards women, workers, Indians, and the poor. And now that the court uses the same reasoning and tactics to put Québec in its place, you express outrage at the fact that we have protected ourselves by an escape clause.

Your outrage is selective.

If I read you right, we Québécois are acceptable to the rest of the country as long as we play by the rules, lose in overtime, and shake hands afterwards. We must always remain good sports and come back to fight another day. Well, you are in for a disappointment, my Canadian friend. A big disappointment.

You are willing to concede some French, even a lot of French, but the Québec landscape still should look and sound like a Canadian landscape. After all, as you so diplomatically remind us, this land is still your land and no amount of misbehaving on our part should be allowed to change the geography of the Dominion.

Am I exaggerating? Of course I am. You are not longing for the good old days when all the best maids were French and the butlers, as well as the bosses, were English. Those days will not return although you would like to have us acknowledge all the adjustments you had to make to catch up to the twentieth century.

How could we not be grateful at your rehabilitation? Is it not true that some of you even permitted us the right to self-determination, including the right to secede and form our own country?

Yes, here I am thanking you on my knees for not behaving like the whites of South Africa, French Algerians or the Chinese in Tibet. How nice, how ... *les mots me manquent* ... bloody nice on your part, old chap. But you never told me that you wanted to be evaluated on the South Africa–China human rights and dignity spectrum. If you insist, we can and we will accommodate you. And while we are on the subject of gratitude, how should I interpret your repeated statement that there "has been an increased responsiveness to Quebec and its demands since the Quiet Revolution." What "responsivenesss"? Do you mean that every time we manage to have a share of what all Canadians are entitled to, these are mere bones you are throwing to us. My friend, we are not dogs eating at the table because of your generosity. We are citizens and taxpayers. We hold Canadian passports. Or do you mean to say that all this is simply the result of your "responsiveness"?

How dare you write of your "openness, of which the willingness to accept the results of the 1980 referendum without flinching is a perfect example." It must be an error. You did not actually write these words. You mean to tell us that we should be grateful to you for having accepted the idea that we could have a referendum. I am sorry that we did not ask permission! *Je crois rêver. C'est le monde à l'envers.* I can only suggest that you do not walk around Québec spouting this kind of argument. It will not help our evolving dialogue and, frankly, I am not sure there is much to talk about with someone who tells me not only that I should be grateful, but how and in what ways I should express my gratitude.

Again I cannot find the words to express my outrage and I return to your third letter in the hope of finding something hidden between the lines that would give me a different impression. But I find that you deny that my outrage can have any validity even before I express it. With a sense of moral superiority you tell me:

Do not take the easy way out, filing these letters away as the hue and cry of an outsider, *un étranger*, who refuses to understand. Listen, for once, to the words of a friend who would listen to yours, and accept that you have no more claim to a monopoly on virtue and truth than he has.

You actually wrote these words. Therefore we should get a few things straight. I will take whatever way out I want if I need to. But who do you think you are with your new-found national identity. You want rules? I will give you rules. First, never lecture people on dialogue and *savoir-vivre*. Say what you want to say and leave it to me to react. And remember that you are the new kid on the nationalist block. If you want to talk about English Canada's national interest, that is fine with me. But don't pretend you are doing it from a superior position. *Non, mais franchement!* Someone who writes in such a way is surely no friend, and so from now on I suggest you stop calling me one.

Second, I will indeed consider your admonitions as the maunderings of an outsider and *un étranger*. It will be safer if I charge these digressions to your status as a foreigner. We Québécois have little difficulty dealing with foreigners. We take them as they are. It is with our friends that problems usually arise. Third, I will not listen to this mixture of ponderous half-lies and non-truths. I do not even need a claim on virtue to do so: simple common sense and intellectual honesty will suffice.

If dialogue is never easy, as you say, you make it especially difficult by resorting to rhetorical strategems which I could un-doubtedly consider offensive and insulting if it were not for the fact that we Québécois have made considerable use of them in the past. It is ironic to be served one's favourite medicine. The taste is sour and the aftertaste made even more bitter by the knowledge that it is done intentionally. It is especially well done when you proclaim at the outset that any attempt on our part to "react instinctively" to your accusation of betrayal will be considered mere "recriminations" on our part. It does not leave us much room to manoeuvre. You also proclaim that you "do not hate us" – again, mighty decent of you, old chap! – nor do you consider our relationship to be one of "conqueror-conquered." I am reassured to find out that our relationship is "nothing else than that between two free and equal parties."

You will not succeed in painting me into a corner by denying me the tools that come with being a minority. If I want to react instinctively, I will, especially now that you are doing the same. If I want to remind you that there is no greater injustice than to treat two non-equals as equals, I will do so. Nor will I be prevented from pointing out that the English Canadian claim to the usefulness of the French fact in distinguishing Canada from the United States – a claim you yourself endorsed – is paternalistic and insulting. If you want to use my instinctive reaction against me and as a sign of my inability to understand anything about English Canada, then go ahead.

Who ever said, "Make my day!"

When I read and reread some of your letters – and believe me I did – at times they seemed to me a plea for us to recognize the blood and tears of the "white man's burden," your burden, in bringing political civilization to Québec. Is it not true, you proclaim, that Medicare, the Canada Pension Plan, Petro-Canada, Air Canada, the National Energy Policy and the Canada Council were all brought to us care of the federal government? I will grant you that indeed many of these additions to the Canadian political and economic landscape were brought about through the policies and moneys of the central government. But so what, I am tempted to say. Do you think for a minute that Petro-Canada is a product of a streak of genius and generosity in Canadian federalism?

You are getting old my friend. You, the Canadian Left, the NDP, the Canadian Labour Congress, and *This Magazine* are getting incredibly old. I am no expert on Canada or English Canada, but I have the impression you have been left behind by what is happening in this country. I am all for a romantic vision of the Cape Breton miner, the Red Deer rancher, and the Kamloops lumberman, but this is romance not reality. Do not take your anger out on us. We are not part of your problem; we are only searching for our own solution.

Maybe you are right to point out that things will never be the same between us. No longer will I be able to trust your description of the changes taking place in the land – its strengths, its ingrained wisdom, and its sorrows. In the past, I never assumed you had any hidden agenda when you were telling me about Canada and Canadians. I enjoyed discovering how people in Nova Scotia, Saskatchewan, or Ontario dealt with their challenges. We had so many things in common that it was easy for me to understand. English Canadians and their rapport to the land and the culture, this is what has always fascinated me in Canada. If you are so wrong and out of touch with Québec, how wrong are you when you tell me about Canada and Canadians.

You are locked in a time-warp, somewhere between the golden sixties and the next century. We have nice memories of the sixties, especially in Québec: marches down Sainte-Catherine Street, sit-ins at Murray's restaurant (although why we wanted to eat there in the first place, I will never know), the American consulate, rallies at the Paul-Sauvé Arena, a few bombs. A package of Gitanes, Leo Ferré in the background, and endless debates as to whether or not Mao was right and Fidel wrong. We talked and you listened. You liked us then. You always like us when we talk. When we act, disappointment is inevitable. We failed you in so many ways that I hesitate to list them. We failed you by bringing back the Union Nationale in 1966 and again when we elected Trudeau in 1968 and refused to see the light at the end of the NDP tunnel in 1972 and 1974. We failed you by not winning the provincial election in 1970 and by winning it in 1976 after having hidden our separatist option. We let you down in the 1980 referendum and then again by moving against some of the most corporatist and right-wing unions on the planet in 1982. We could have provided the guiding light of progressive egalitarianism. Instead, we have but a French version of the capitalist ethic to offer.

We know failure like the palm of our hand.

Even when we failed, we manage to fail you. Not like the French, the "real" French that is. *Ah, les Français!* They really know their way around red wine, Camembert, and failures – mostly revolutions. May 68! That was the way to go, with a bang. But we Québécois, we do not even have the decency to know when our number is up and when our time has come ... and gone. *Nous persistons et nous signons*, as Jacques Brel would have said.

Maybe next time, we will measure up to your expectations and keep up with the Ortegas in Nicaragua. If and when we have our very own socialist revolution, you will be the first to know, and we will drink wine again in the cafés of Montréal. But do not hold your breath. I am afraid that we are bound to disappoint you time after time. But what you consider to be a disappointment is often seen by us as just another step, one which could have been bigger and bolder but one we can live with. You quote *The Decline of the American Empire* as the symbol of our *déchéance* into a world of private desires. Rarely has a film aged so rapidly. Rarely has a *déchéance* been so short-lived. In 1989, the film to see is *Jésus de Montréal*, also by Denys Arcand, a tale of solidarity and truth. Apparently it received an official cold shoulder at the Toronto Film Festival where the big hit this year was a documentary about General Motors. *Autre pays, autre moeurs.*

You need not worry so much about us, about who we are and where we are going. We never had our own business class and, since no one has yet figured out how to do without one, I prefer one chaired by Bernard Lamarre of Lavalin, Michel Gaucher who has just bought Steinberg, and Bernard Lemaire of Cascades. Do not get me wrong. It is not the pride of knowing we can produce our own capitalists – some knowledge you can live without – it is the satisfaction of discovering how well integrated, like it or not, these people are in the social and cultural fabric of Québec society. They could not survive one minute outside of the Québec network. The smile you see on my face comes from knowing they cannot make a move without the support of the Caisse de dépôt and the Caisses populaires.

You should have tried the Caisse de dépôt experiment yourselves twenty years ago when Québec decided to go it alone from the Canada Pension Plan. By now you could have bought back Canada from the Americans instead of spending so much of your resources trying to buy a piece of Atlanta real estate. Or you should think about creating your own Fonds de solidarité, managed by the Québec Federation of Labour and soon to become the largest equity holder in Québec. So you see why I am not worried. I have no illusions as to the motives of this new business class. They want airplanes and condominiums. But to get them they have to work somewhat harder at building a consensus. In addition, I do not even have to convince them of their Québécois identity. English Canada is doing it for me.

CHEER UP, YOU'VE WON!

Is it putting it too simplistically to say that you have won? Perhaps, but I have wanted from the beginning to keep it simple. Throughout your letters I sensed the feelings and read the words of someone who has been pushed too far for too long. Why not say openly: "We have had enough." Of course this would put you squarely in the camp of those English Canadians who believe that French should be eradicated from the face of this land. Not nice company, I agree. Until today, you could find comfort in the belief that your position – yours and that of the progressive, liberal, and open-minded segments of English Canadian opinion – was free of bigotry. You stood alone and thus could survey the battlefield where most of us fought through our prejudices and incomprehensions. Oh, what a lovely war it must have been. In one easy stroke, you could dismiss the extremists in both camps, have the intellectual pleasure of endless arguments with us, and have the satisfaction of not being in the same camp as the rednecks from Edmonton and the unilinguals from Fredericton. Of course, in the end you always chose your own side and curiously enough never came out on ours, but except for this small detail, which we all chose to ignore, your attitude was always one of comprehension, fortitude, and compassion.

The war is over and you won, or more precisely your "strange bedfellows" won it for you. I am not sure of their reaction now that you have decided to fly to the defence of their victory. But that is another matter. You have to come to grips with the fact that in 1760, 1837, 1867, 1942, and 1980, it is your side and not mine which has won. Mind you, this is what those rednecks and English unilinguals have been saying from the beginning. It is time you caught up with your own history and, if I read your letters correctly, this is precisely what you have started to do. At least, that is how I interpret your poignant "Things will never be the same." Will you believe me when I say that I sincerely hope things will never be the same. I am even prepared to sustain a series of pernicious, sometimes infantile and always caustic attacks on your part, if they can help prevent the past from repeating itself. In the end, we will both benefit; in fact there are already some benefits. No longer do I have to find excuses for your paternalistic attitudes and you need claim no solidarity with our chauvinistic laws. Last weekend, the federal NDP reneged on its support for Meech Lake, sending all of its twelve ... or is it seventeen Québec factions and wings back into oblivion. The Liberal Party is thinking of doing the same. One stroke for "Truth in advertising," you might say.

As someone who has had to live for years with a host of reactionary, xenophobic, ethnocentric and occasionally openly racist Québec nationalists; let me welcome you to the nationalist club. A word of warning for you: it is not easy living and you will soon come to miss your former detachment. Over the last twenty years, I have spent more time arguing with people who insisted on calling themselves nationalists and independentists than with those on the other side. Now, it is your turn. You have chosen your camp and I sincerely hope you can live with it. I do not say this because it will offer me some good cheap shots – and they're always the best – in our continuing dialogue, but because I feel it will clear the air. Maybe there is some justice after all. For every time you bring out Camille Laurin, the "psychotic father" of Bill 101, Adrien Arcand, the fascist leader of the 1930s, or Maurice Duplessis as Québec nationalists of good standing, I will be able to point out that the English Canadian camp includes Mayor Jones of Moncton, Bill Vander Zalm of your own province, and industrialist Conrad Black. And you must now take responsibility for Jean Chrétien.

After years of hesitation, English Canadian "progressives" have finally come home to roost. No longer will they pretend to stay aloof from their own society. In the past, they saw themselves mostly as social-democrats, Marxists, unionists, regionalists, feminists, or environmentalists. If necessary, they would also claim a Canadian identity but they used it mostly to differentiate themselves from Americans. It was on the basis of these self descriptions that English Canadian intellectuals hoped to join forces with their Québec counterparts. Your strategy was a simple one and it almost worked. You made no open claim on Canada and you refused to align yourself with a parochial "English Canadianness," and in return you expected us to keep our nationalism under control. Why not admit it? For years, we have been using one another. In our case it is evident. You always provided the perfect excuse and the appropriate scapegoat. But you did the same. For all those years, you put up with our nationalism and its extravagant claims and wild accusations thinking that it was an adolescent phase. It was a prerequisite to socialism, you argued forcefully, a rite of passage on the road to a more global consciousness. Did you not secretly hope all this Québec agitation would push your various governments, provincial or federal, in a more social-democratic direction. I know you did not need us to lead the way: the Saskatchewan NDP long preceded the Quiet Revolution. But for some reason the process stalled in the 1950s and the Québec menace provided a new impetus for change.

We were so proud to be regarded as the harbingers of progress. We knew it was not true but said nothing because your view of us was so flattering and comforting. We were not just separatists or nationalists, you said. Behind this façade and rhetoric lay a more universal longing. One day we would emerge. As someone who never went in for flag waving, Paul-Sauvé Arena meetings, and letters to the editors protesting unilingual services aboard Air Canada, I can only testify to our satisfaction at knowing that one day it would all be over. As the Idi Amins, the Khmer Rouges, and the Gadhafis of this world used nationalism as part of their genocidal actions, we were grateful for your insistence on the "progressive" nature of our nationalism. We did not trust it ourselves and, if you said it was politically correct, then it must be true.

Our nationalism has been proclaimed dead so many times that we are now convinced it can survive any crisis. It even managed to survive a brief flirtation with 1980s neo-conservatism. The market maniacs who so dominated the Bourassa government between 1986 and 1989 are gone, victims of the mess they created and their desire for more money and better limousines. The 1989 nurses'strike with its unprecedented level of popular support blew them away. Québec is back on track.

Ever since 1960, you have forced yourself to make excuses for us. And now you are tired. So are we. We are what we are. Thank you for the idealized image, but we can live without it.

It is about time you began building a similarly idealized vision of English Canada, one that does not always get bogged down in self-depreciation. Do not waste any more time by substituting primitive anti-Québec feelings for your primitive anti-American ones. It will lead you nowhere.

You have finally come to the conclusion that one cannot be an environmentalist, a socialist, or a feminist in the abstract, outside the realm of a particular society. These political programs only make sense if they are supported by an encompassing collective definition, one that reflects the real world. The writing is on the wall everywhere: think globally and act locally. This is what they are doing in Estonia, in Poland, in Hungary, China, and Brazil. If this is how it is going to be in English Canada from now on, so be it. I know full well you will not believe me – and why should you – but I wish you luck and pray for your success. I do it for your sake and also because we will all benefit. I dream of the day when we can borrow ideas, initiatives, innovations, and precedents from Toronto and not just complain that our unemployment rate in Montréal is twice as high. It has been such a long time since we have heard anything "nice" about Canada, something other than your constant recriminations over Meech Lake.

I hope I am reading you correctly since it is only through this new English Canadian nationalism that we, Canadians and Québécois, will be able to move forward, sometimes together and at other times apart. There is so much to talk about other than whether or not we are behaving according to your plans. You are quite right in pointing out the limitations imposed by our own self-centred nationalism. After close to thirty years, we have milked it to the bone. We need a new influx of ideas and new partners in our "dialogue" and I believe English Canada, especially if people like you will take part, could provide the partner we so desperately need. If I am right, it is going to be fascinating to watch. Imagine a whole nation, close to twenty million strong, coming to life before our very eyes. There is so much you can teach us and the rest of the world. How to deal with the Americans for example and how to make sure a culture can prosper while sharing a language and so many values with a powerful neighbour.

There is much we can learn from you, but this is not the fundamental reason why I have always wanted to find out about English Canada: it interests me. My sense of solidarity with English Canada evaporates when you force me to put it in a federalist framework but, if you do not insist that I sing the national anthem or add a paragraph in praise of the Great Canadian Dialogue, it will be there when you need it. I say all this knowing perfectly well that Québec and Québécois are in for a rough time. We have taken you for granted, less than that even, for so long, the awakening will be difficult. But, do we have any choice? We have outlived the usefulness of our respective self-delusions.

Allow me to jump the gun, dream about our future dialogue. It will have a "we-them" quality which we are not used to. You have always refused to say "we" and have always looked at us as part of your Canadian "we." New words will have to be invented to describe what we feel and think about one another. So far, I have not particularly liked what you had to say about us. I believe you to be wrong on most counts. But at least, you are talking.

BETRAYAL OF OUR POLITICS

You are surprised that we are trying to have it both ways: bilinguism in Canada and unilinguism in Québec, Meech Lake to protect our distinctiveness and the Free Trade Agreement to open up Canada to the United States, an insistence on telling you how to organize yourselves but horror when you tell us how to run our affairs. It is tempting to ask where you were before 1988. It is also tempting to point out that Meech Lake is a federal initiative to modify the Canadian Constitution, that Bill 178 is a reaction to a Canadian Supreme Court decision based on the 1982 Constitution and that the Free Trade Agreement was achieved only because the two most important economic regions of the country, Ontario and the West, saw fit that it should come about. It is all very Canadian, would you not agree? Take away the 1982 Constitution and its American-inspired Bill of Rights, take away the National Energy Policy and the resurgence of the West, and there is no Meech Lake, no Bill 178, and no ·Free Trade Agreement.

May I also point out that your insinuation about our lack of fair play and respect for the rules of decency is out of order. We had and continue to have little choice. Bill 101 was adopted in 1978. It complied with the rules as they existed at the time. It is the federal government with the complicity of the provincial premiers of English Canada who changed the rules in 1982. I was shocked to realize that you do not even mention the fact that the driving force behind the adoption of your beloved Charter of Rights was to put Québec in its proper linguistic place. Another case of selective memory, I suppose. The intentions of your new-found bedfellows were not as pure as you like to think.

In the next years, the courts invalidated several sections of the Charte de la langue française and we fully complied with these rulings. This will probably come as a surprise to you, but we went so far as to change some of the provisions of the *Charte* democratically. In 1985, we elected a Liberal government which promptly gave the English-speaking minority back some of its privileges. We do not need the courts to tell us how to behave in a democracy and you to remind us that "we have proven supremely indifferent to questions of minority language rights or freedom of expression." Beware! You are now dangerously close to the old argument that somewhere, deep in the soul of every French Canadian, lies a reactionary and a fascist. I know the argument well. It still surfaces once in a while in places like McGill, your old alma mater.

Basically, your argument is only the old, old argument that we want to have our cake and eat it too.

Daniel Latouche

If you detect a certain disappointment behind this statement you are right. I was extremely disappointed in hearing it from you. From you of all people. I was not expecting arguments directed at our lack of partisan savoir vivre. You could have questioned our strategy. I happen to believe it is a dangerous way of building a strong industrial base. These would have been difficult arguments to refute. Or you could have pointed out that not all means are acceptable to redress a situation or that there are people in Canada worse off than the Québécois. No, you choose to fault us because we insist in getting our economic rewards for sharing in the great Canadian federation. Is there a rule book we do not know about which indicates that irrational regional pressures and blatant partisan maneuvring are not options open to us? You wanted us in the tent, doing what people in the tent are supposed to do, so do not complain about the smell. We do not yet have the class of Bay Street or the clout of Edmonton, but we are learning. We had good teachers.

Of course, Québec wants to have its cake and eat it too, and so does the rest of Canada. Now that the federal cake is shrinking, the addition of one more provincial mouth to feed – a loud one, I'll grant you that – does not simplify matters. Yes, I know we are not drowning in gratitude. We should say thank you and perhaps apologize for the unabashedly political way in which we went after the cf-18 deal. It was pure patronage. But if someone should be ashamed, it is not English Canada, but Québec for having to live with such rules. And we will do it again and again. We can live with the shame; we have done so for a long time. There will never be enough days in the calendar for us to get even. What did I say? I am wrong. We do not want to get even. We want to get ahead.

And at the same time we want to get angry. Our anger will not subside. It will grow with each new bit of cake. Mind you, few people here would have paid any attention to the cf-18 deal or any of the others, if the rest of the country had not insisted that it be considered as the last concession, the final down payment to the nagging Québec wife. We have seen so many deals come and go, (mostly go) that one more injustice would add little to the balance of things. It is Ottawa and the federal government who define the rules of the game. Not so long ago these rules were useful in persuading reluctant Québécois that they should stick with their Canadian cake rather than go on their own. At the time of the referendum the same CF-18 planes – their assembly this time – were promised to Québec by politicians urging a "No" vote.

This line of argument was used during the referendum debate. Do not leave Canada, we were told, or you will lose your chance to have your cake and eat it too. You wanted a country based on accounting practices, on similar bookkeeping procedures from coast to coast, on a "winner-take-all" approach. You've got it.

I am not dreaming these things up, nor am I dreaming the fact that you deliberately choose to ignore them. We are used to this kind of reaction from the rest of the country. We saw it in the nineteenth century, in the 1940s, six months ago, and last week. We have seen you do it repeatedly, as if it were the Canadian way. Ever since Newfoundland joined Confederation you have used the same argument whenever there was a possibility of their escaping their under-development. You never miss a chance of doing it to the Northern people, to the West, or to the Acadians. Yes, we have learned the great Canadian way. Every time we pass "Go," we will collect our collective $ 200. The game is only starting.

And please, do not tell us that this tit-for-tat attitude does not contribute to the dialogue between our two communities. What dialogue?

M. LAKE AND THE CANADIAN SOUL

Apparently M. Lake has profoundly affected and insulted you. You do not like the distinct society clause, nor do you appreciate the fact that provincial premiers will now have something to say about Supreme Court justices and senators. The idea that provinces will be able to opt out of federal programs and that unanimity will be required before the Yukon is admitted to our select Canadian Club sends shock waves through your democratic spine. Have I forgotten anything? Yes, you also despise the secret and closed way in which it was approved. I agree! Can we talk of something else? You want me to add to your indictment of M. Lake? No problem! There are many things you forgot. You might have added that this entire distinct society façade is a front, an affront to our political culture. We all know it has absolutely no legal meaning and that Québec has no need of such a clause. It will poison further the atmosphere between our two nations for years to come, as we will come to expect great rewards from what is being presented to us as a great concession on your part.

M. Lake is no hero to us. It is only because of your objections that we have developed some sympathy towards him. If English Canada is against him, there must be something good about the guy.

Each day this argument gains converts in Québec and I am angry about it. What a waste of time and energy. Your attitude is forcing us to take Meech Lake seriously. Our professional activists, those whose job it is to find something new about English Canada to pick on, are hard at work. We will now hear about Meech Lake for years to come. What happens if Meech Lake is prevented from landing on our pristine constitutional shores? Nothing! Except that for years to come, the land will be drowned under the lament, "On veut Meech Lake." What a prospect. And the next time around Meech Lake will be even more ambiguous. Do you think for a second that Québec will separate from Canada because you refused to recognize our symbolic existence? We might be emotional or even irrational, but we are not that ridiculous.

Sovereignty does not depend on such an argument. Independence has less and less to do with you and the way you are treating us. The words "les maudits anglais" do not turn anybody on anymore. Of course our nationalist politicians will go on making speeches about how badly the Anglais are treating us. They know the script by heart and it always brings a few nostalgic tears for the good old days when our fight was over bilingual stamps and French services in Kapuskasing.

M. Lake! Will you please make up your mind. First, it was Manitoba, then New Brunswick and then the NDP. If you do not like M. Lake, then kill him and let us get it over with. Spare us the hesitations and maybe yes and maybe no. Spare us the blackmail about not deserving to be recognized as a distinct society. Spare yourself the dishonour of having to argue that Meech Lake is dangerous because of the use we might make of it.

How does it feel to hide behind the skirts of two of the most parochial and reactionary premiers of Canada? What about your favourite argument about the lack of vision of Canadian provincial premiers? In this case, it is two of the most provincial of these premiers who are about to save you and your country from the grip of Meech Lake. Talk of strange bedfellows. I am reminded of Woody Allen's famous quote: "I don't want to become a member of a club that would accept me as a member." I am not sure if I want to be party to a country which deals with serious constitutional matters in such a frivolous way. Can you imagine how it looks in London, Tokyo, or Frankfurt? Here is Canada, an active player on the world scene, a country which tries to tell others how to behave, a member of the Group of Seven, now stalled in its constitutional development because Manitoba and New Brunswick are having second thoughts? Do something, my friend, if not for your sake, for mine.

LEAVE "NOS ANGLAIS" ALONE

In your third letter, you invoke an interesting explanation for our recent behaviour: "Correct me if I am wrong, *cher ami*, but I detect a simple desire for vengeance, for paying the Anglos back for their sins of omission and commission, in your current outpouring of emotion." Well, I will take you up on your offer, *mon cher ami*, and correct you. Rest assured: there is no desire for vengeance on our part, especially not over the question of language. If we wanted to get back at you on the language front, it would take too long and would require too much energy. Sorry, but no thanks. To get even with English Canada? You could not even get forty people to march behind this banner.

You are wrong, so totally wrong that again I doubt that you could be right on other points. Let us begin with the facts – we can always deal with the interpretation later. You suggest that we offer "some tacit recognition of the legitimacy of the language of the shrinking anglophone minority." Here you are wrong and you are out of date. First, we are not interested in "tacit" recognition and I am sure Québec anglophones are not either. They want a real recognition of their community, its institutions, its traditions, its culture. Tacit recognition is the way you have been treating French-speaking minorities for a century. Oh they have "tacit" recognition, but nothing else. Each year we spend a few hundred millions of dollars on the institutions of the anglophone community, more I might add than all the provinces and the federal government spend each year for the institutions of French Canada. We have always done so and will continue to do so. We leave to you the dubious honour of maintaining a comparative accounting of the treatment of our respective minorities. Some of us do not like it but McGill, the Protestant School Board, the Montreal General Hospital, and the Centaur Theatre are part of our heritage and will continue to be so. Even Alliance Quebec is supported by the taxes of francophones.

Second, your use of the word "shrinking" to describe what is happening to the anglophone minority implies that it went down, let us say, from 40 or 30 per cent of the total Québec population to its present level of 16 or 15 per cent. Let me reassure that your dear old Westmount is not disappearing. Of course, in the past, one might have got the impression that

Québec was divided about half and half between French and English. English was everywhere. It no longer is. As for the relative size of the anglophone minority, it has been in the 15 to 20 per cent range as far back as we care to remember.

Even with all of its present difficulties, the anglophone community is able to attract newcomers, even French-speaking Québécois. At least two out of three, and I suspect it is closer to three out of four, immigrants to Québec eventually join this community. Can you imagine the same proportion of Asian immigrants assimilating to the French-speaking minority in Vancouver? Well, this is precisely what is happening in Montréal. In recent years, this note of assimilation has been somewhat reduced because of Bill 101, but, with each attack on the language laws, we move back towards the situation that existed in the 1960s when 90 to 95 per cent of newcomers joined the English side. We thought for a while that by sending them to French schools, they would integrate into the French community. They learn the language, but for them it is but another requirement on the road to citizenship.

Your letters indicate that you know about this situation, but again you choose to ignore the facts. Why? You are also aware that one of the reasons for the demographic downturn, as small as it is, of the anglophone community lies in its massive exodus from Québec. You even know that it is not really an exodus but a case of non-replacement. Québec's anglophone community has always been highly mobile, but suddenly English Canadians have stopped coming to replace those leaving. I will not argue about the reasons. I know very well what they are: those who left found the atmosphere unbearable and those who did not come want to live in a culturally attractive environment. The same reasons apply to French Canadians who come back to Québec and to the Québécois who are not attracted to Moose Jaw or Toronto.

More important still, you are confusing the English language and the English-speaking minority. No one, not even the strongest supporters of Alliance Quebec suggests that the English language is threatened in Québec. Even to think along these lines is ridiculous. English is alive and well in Québec. What Alliance Quebec has been complaining about is the erosion of their community institutions. I believe them to be wrong in this regard, but I will readily admit it to be a question of perception. English-speaking Quebecers, especially those of Anglo-Saxon origin, feel that what used to make their community so livable and challenging is being eroded. They are probably right. They used to be on top and recognized for the excellence of their achievements in business, the arts, community services and science. Now they have become irrelevant to the rest of Canada and treated as a minority by the Québécois. I know what they are going through. When they insist that we recognize how wonderful their adjustment has been, they are reacting like minorities everywhere. I suspect that they will never get used to that position. We certainly did not. They have retained control of all of their institutions and I will spare you the litany of how well we treat them. Nevertheless I am surprised that you do not even mention the fact that one of the components of Québec nationalism of which we can be proudest is the way we treat our minority.

What is the use of being so knowledgeable about Québec society and so sympathetic to our objectives, if you make no use of this knowledge. Of course, it is much easier to argue that Québec nationalism needs some "maturing" and that the best way to show for it is to extend a "fraternal hand to that minority". I am tempted to tell you to take care of your own nationalism, your own minorities, and your own fraternal hand, and we will take care of ours. As a matter of fact, we have been doing a good job on this front for thirty years while your record is abysmal and not getting any better. When you tell us now that the way you treat the French Canadian farmers of Saint-Boniface will depend on our treatment of Westmount, you are not helping your case. I do not know what to make of such *mauvaise foi*.

I will grant you that at the outset the free trade debate passed almost unnoticed in Québec. Most Québécois know nothing of the anguish it has created in English Canada. Those who know either do not care or have little sympathy. This state of ignorance has nevertheless one advantage: if Québécois were aware that you are mad at them for having voted for the free trade party, they would in turn be furious. Most Québécois are convinced that free trade is a federal initiative supported by the English Canadian community. Most of them are convinced that they voted correctly – as was expected of them. The pro–free trade voices from English Canada were all saying the same thing: free trade is good for the country, free trade will bring us prosperity, no free trade and we are doomed. According to most in English Canada, free trade was for winners. And the Québécois surely want to be on the side of the winners. Few people will explain the vote this way. They prefer pompous words about our new feeling of confidence. Nonsense. Most Québécois voted for free trade because the *Puissants* and the Powerful of English Canada said they should.

And even this explanation is a bit too rational considering how little impact the free trade issue had by itself. There was simply no room for us in the "Save Canada" movement of the Anti–Free Trade Coalition. I am being too polite again. The more we listened to some of the arguments of the coalition, the more we felt a sudden urge to join the Mulroney campaign. I am not talking here of the "If it's bad for Ontario, then it must be good for Québec" argument. No, I am referring to the constant references to the inevitable demise of Ottawa's control over the provinces which would follow free trade. I sat through a number of evenings where somber-looking artists and union members from English Canada tried to persuade me that free trade could mean a new surge of decentralization in favour of the provincial barons, a degradation in the quality of the Canadian culture and a threat to our great Canadian institutions.

Not once did I hear a "dump free trade" advocate point out that free trade was dangerous because it posed a special menace to the originality, dynamism, and distinctiveness of the Québec culture. Not once was I told of the dangers to the bilingual and bicultural nature of this country. Did anyone ever mention that the free trade deal could cause havoc in Québec-Canada relations or that it would make it impossible for these relations to evolve towards greater equality. No, you were not interested in these questions. What suddenly worried you was the posibility that you might lose your Québec market. I even had to listen to the argument that free trade and Meech Lake were a Québec conspiracy. You are not far from thinking along those lines yourself. English Canadians of the liberal and progressive school should consider themselves lucky that Québécois did not pay much attention to the free trade debate. If they had, their support would have been real and unanimous.

You claim that your feelings towards us "have in no way been altered because of the election." Your bitterness is directed towards the "Claude Charrons and Jacques Parizeaus of this world, towards a whole stratum of self-proclaimed Québécois nationalists whose cynicism with regard to our interests can only breed passionate hostility in reply." Why this anger? Do not tell me you share in this fairy-tale vision that the Québec separatists supported free trade because it was another blow to Ottawa and Canada? Few "separatists" hold this view. As a matter of fact, many of the people you quote favoured free trade before they became separatists. And, while we are on the subject, do you think for a minute that the free trade deal would have been stopped if more Québécois had voted Liberal and more of the rest of the country Conservative? Can you imagine a single anti–free trade proponent standing up and saying that we cannot have free trade since the Québécois voted against it and it is part of the bicultural deal that we not proceed on important matters without the support of both national communities. Of course not.

You are right in pointing out that the free trade deal is embedded in a neo-conservative model of the worst kind (if you remember well, this was also my argument on the Supreme Court's ruling on commercial signs in Québec). And thank you for pointing out how much such a deal goes against the grain of the "core values" of English Canada and its distinctiveness. I happen to believe that what is bad for English Canada is often equally bad for Québec. Consequently, my worry is genuine. But why do you assume that those of us who supported free trade – "supported" is too strong a word – did so only because of electoral reasoning of the worst kind?

The question is one of "modèle de société." What is the best way for any given group to adopt a *modèle* which corresponds to its "core values"? Your basic preference is for a universal, world-government solution. I respect that. Nevertheless I disagree with your premise that "sovereignty of the Hobbesian variety is of diminishing importance in the late twentieth century." On the contrary, it is more important than ever, for a small society like ours in any case, and not just because it is a second-best strategy in view of a more "international" one. I could hold back a smile when I read that in the absence of a world polity, national boundaries continue to provide the basis for communitarian endeavours, and for progressive over reactionary values. René Lévesque and Jacques Parizeau could not have said it any better.

Our strategic analysis is different. We also want less of a "dog-eat-dog" society but we happen to believe that the free trade deal with the United States does not seriously threaten the *modèle* we have been building over the years. I am not entirely certain of this and so I hesitated over free trade. But the alternative, assuming it was a real one, of a world-wide liberalization under a GATT agreement, would be a catastrophe for Québec and will remain one until we take our own (very small) seat at the table of nation-states.

There is much to disagree with in your presentation of the free trade issue, notably when you state so categorically that a rejection of the deal "would have symbolized our opting in a more progressive direction," but this is not what is at stake here. The arguments that were used by the Anti–Free Trade Coalition, the alternative they proposed and the reinforcement of the core values of the English Canadian model of society, all lead us to believe that a more international solution, even if it implies the United States, was best for Québec. For all of Québec and not just our new entrepreneurs. Of course, if we had reconstructed the country along different constitutional lines a long time ago, the reasoning would have been a different one. But we did not.

INDIGNATION AT OUR IGNORANCE

You are on much better ground in your argument when you despair at the Québécois' special mixture of ignorance, intolerance, and benign neglect concerning all things English Canadian. In this area, things are not getting any better, they are getting worse. Your example of the free trade debate is not a good case in point. Nobody, but nobody, in Québec was aware of the threat this deal presented to your identity. Your example is the wrong one, but the point is well taken.

It is your explanation of English Canadian nationalism that is certainly the most interesting part of your letters, the part that should be required reading for all Québécois. Reading the rest though would not help our future dialogue. May I suggest at the start, however, that you are in part to blame for the Québécois attitude (note that I said "in part"). First, for years you maintained the fiction that English Canada did not exist, could not exist, and should not exist as a distinct cultural identity. I understand very well the geo-political reasoning behind this self-denial. It allowed you to maintain the fiction that any political reconstruction of Canada along bi-national lines was doomed from the start, since one of the two supporting collective entities was entirely a figment of our imagination. For years, we wanted you to exist. Maybe, we wanted it too much, and this explains why you resisted any recognition of yourself. Of course, we were not entirely disinterested in the fact of existence. As a matter of fact, we were not disinterested at all. It would have served us well if we could have convinced you. This is what André Laurendeau, whose support for bilingualism you are so fond of quoting, was trying to do. His failure was our failure, and the reason he is still so much respected in Québec, by federalists, separatists, and Marxists alike, is because he continued to try to persuade English Canada that it existed as a nation.

For years, you kept telling us that there were so few things that distinguished English Canada from the United States that you needed us to make you feel different. How could we resist an argument so sweet to our ears. We wanted recognition and although you made sure that we would not get it, you also made sure that we were given the best substitute, flattery. And did we go for it. For years – if this is beginning to sound like an incantation, that is precisely what it is supposed to be – you kept reminding us that English Canada did not exist because Manitobans were as distinct from Albertans as Québécois from Frenchmen. Your regional, ethnic, cultural differences were such that to force you within the same cauldron made little sense. I remember it too well. Your statement and then our feeble attempt to convince you that Gaspésiens were really very different from Montréalais and that a Québécois from the Saguenay considered a neighbour from the Lac-Saint-Jean a perfect stranger. Of course, we did not believe it, but we were ready to use almost any piece of false logic to convince you of your own existence. If you were willing to play such a simplistic game, we would try to beat you at it.

In the end, we gave in. Again you won by flattering us by

insisting that the Québécois were something else altogether. Our difference was better, so much more different than your difference. We were a real nation. We had roots, a sense of collective self, a history to share, heroes and Maurice Richard. You had nothing of the sort. In short, you were *incolore, inodore et sans saveur*.

We finally agreed to bring colour, sound, and flavour to Canada. We agreed to serve as your distinctiveness. You wanted your national-ethnic Disneyland. We were going to be it. You wanted to be able to tell Americans that you had a "société distincte" amongst you; we agreed to satisfy you. And now you have the *culot* of turning around and telling us that your distinctiveness is equal to ours. Sorry, it won't wash. We are the Minority. We have been practising it for two centuries. The British, and even the French before them, recognized it and acted accordingly. Who are you to change the rules of the game now that you realize there is some advantage being someone's minority? Of course, there is some advantage. How do you think we managed to survive for the last centuries? But, as we say in French, "Tes affaires et dans ta cour." (I will leave that for you to figure out!)

Although you might be held responsible for the Québécois indifference towards English Canada with your own attitude towards it, there is really no excuse for such indifference. Contrary to what you so easily assumed, it is not a case of parochial nationalism too happy to focus exclusively on all things "made in Québec" but oblivious to the rest of the word. Clearly, this is what you and the self-proclaimed progressive forces in English Canada have come to believe. It is also what Pierre Trudeau and his friends used to say. Of course, Québec nationalism has had its share of parochialism. Like many others I am ill at ease with some of the manifestations of this sense of belonging: the fleur-de-lys, "Mon pays ce n'est pas un pays," and the "tourtière." Maybe we need such symbols. Maybe every society also needs, somewhere in the back of its collective mind, a belief in its intrinsic superiority. Perhaps, but do not ask me to add to this tradition.

But this is not the point. For a vast majority of Québécois, nationalism has been a progressive force, opening their eyes to what was going on in the rest of the world, forcing them to think about things which until recently were outside their frame of reference. As such, I find it unacceptable that they would not be interested and preoccupied by what is going on in English Canada. Nobody, but absolutely nobody shows any interest. There is a lot of envy of the new pre-eminence of Toronto and the new-found richness of Vancouver. There might even be some resentment, a touch of condescendence, and some amusement, but you will not find any respect or concern. No Québec university offers any course on English Canadian society. A seminar on Toronto's historical development or the economy of the Prairies would be unthinkable. For years, I have tried to organize a conference on English Canada, only to be told it is a non-topic. Things will be different in the future.

Or will they?

If I look around me at the structural forces that are pushing Québec towards greater sovereignty and more interdependence with other nations, I feel confident. If I read the last paragraphs of your last letters, I lose my confidence. You still can see us only as a part of Canada and as a parentheses, as when you acknowledge that there will always be differences between us in the ways we "look on Canada and Québec's place within it." Apparently, you can only envisage us as being "part of." When you think of Québec, you think of "our place within." Worse still when you think of a less atomistic, capitalist, and more communitarian society, you think only of the Canadian one, as defined by English Canada. Maybe you cannot help it but understand my disappointment when your final appeal is for me "to join my efforts to yours."

Quelle tristesse! Tu me permettras de terminer cette réponse dans ma langue. J'arrive assez facilement à m'indigner en anglais, mais la tristesse je la réserve au français. Tristesse parce que tout au long de tes lettres j'ai espéré qu'à la fin tu lancerais un appel à une coexistence pacifique et enrichissante de nos deux nationalismes. Mais non, tu te contentes de m'avertir que dorénavant le nationalisme canadien-anglais va prendre toute la place qui lui revient. Tu choisis de terminer par un "Qu'on se le tienne pour dit" de première qualité.

Quand donc verras-tu qu'on ne peut marcher dans la même direction que si nos chemins sont parallèles et distincts l'un de l'autre?

Moi-aussi j'espère pouvoir reprendre cette conversation sous des jours meilleurs. Je ne vois cependant pas le beau temps venir de la même direction.

Mes amitiés aux Montagnes Rocheuses.

Appendix

KEY POLITICAL EVENTS IN QUEBEC SINCE 1960

1960   Election of the Lesage government; beginning of
            the Quiet Revolution

1962   Student demonstrations against Donald Gordon
            of Canadian National Railways; nationalization of
            power companies in Quebec

1963   FLQ bombings; creation of the Royal Commission
            on Bilingualism and Biculturalism

1964   Queen's visit to Quebec City; violent confronta-
            tions between police and demonstrators

1965   Failure of the Fulton-Favreau formula for consti-
            tutional change

1966   Election of a Union Nationale government

1967   Centennial of Canadian Confederation; de
            Gaulle's "Vive le Québec libre" from the bal-
            cony of Montreal's City Hall

1968–69   Pierre Trudeau becomes leader of the federal
            Liberal Party and prime minister of Canada; for-
            mation of the Parti Québécois headed by René
            Lévesque; language riots in the Montreal suburb
            of Saint-Léonard; march for McGill français

1970	Election of Liberal government headed by Robert Bourassa; the October crisis, the kidnapping of James Cross and Pierre Laporte, and the invocation of the War Measures Act
1971–72	*La Presse* strike; strike of the Common Front; failure of the Victoria Conference to resolve the constitutional log-jam
1974–76	Bill 22 passed by the Bourassa government requiring testing of children for admission to English-language schools
1976	Election of a Parti Québécois government headed by René Lévesque
1977	Bill 101, Charte de la langue française, passed, giving French primacy in Quebec and barring access by new immigrants to English-language schools
1980	Quebec referendum on sovereignty-association; 40 percent vote Yes, 60 per cent No
1980–81	Constitutional negotiations leading to the November 1981 agreement to patriate the Canadian Constitution along with a Charter of Rights and Freedoms; Quebec government alone opposes the package
1982–83	Roll-back of public sector wages in Quebec
1985	Defeat of the Parti Québécois; return of Robert Bourassa and the Liberals to power

1987   Meech Lake Constitutional Accord, recognizing
            Quebec as a distinct society and increasing the
            power of all the provinces relative to Ottawa; the
            Accord requires ratification by Parliament and all
            ten provincial legislatures by June 1990

1988   Conservatives led by Brian Mulroney win the
            "free trade" election, taking 63 of Quebec's 75
            seats; Supreme Court rules on 15 December that
            Bill 101's provisions barring outside signs in lan-
            guages other than French violate the Canadian
            and Quebec charters of rights; the Bourassa gov-
            ernment introduces Bill 178 to override this
            judgment; Manitoba withdraws support for the
            Meech Lake Accord

1989   Opposition to Meech Lake Accord grows in
            English Canada; the Bourassa government is re-
            elected in September 1989 with the PQ, led by
            Jacque Parizeau and strongly committed to Que-
            bec independence, taking 40 per cent of the
            popular vote; four Montreal ridings with anglo-
            phone majorities elect members of the Equality
            Party